Building YOUR Tiny House DREAM

T0003755

Building YOUR Tiny House DREAM

DESIGN AND BUILD A CAMPER-STYLE TINY HOUSE WITH YOUR OWN HANDS

CHRIS SCHAPDICK

AUTHOR OF
THE JOY OF TINY HOUSE LIVING

CRE**A**TIVE
HOMEOWNER®

CRE✲TIVE HOMEOWNER®

Copyright © 2020 by Chris Schapdick and Creative Homeowner

BUILDING YOUR TINY HOUSE DREAM
Editor: Colleen Dorsey
Copy Editor: Laura Taylor
Designer: David Fisk
Indexer: Jay Kreider

ISBN 978-1-58011-847-7

Library of Congress Control Number: 2020935256

We are always looking for talented authors. To submit an idea, please send a brief inquiry to acquisitions@foxchapelpublishing.com.

Printed in China

Current Printing (last digit)
10 9 8 7 6 5 4 3 2 1

Creative Homeowner®, *www.creativehomeowner.com*, is an imprint of New Design Originals Corporation and distributed exclusively in North America by Fox Chapel Publishing Company, Inc., 800-457-9112, 903 Square Street, Mount Joy, PA 17552, and in the United Kingdom by Grantham Book Service, Trent Road, Grantham, Lincolnshire, NG31 7XQ.

All costs related to your tiny home project will vary by project, location, and many other variables; therefore, all costs given in this book should be understood to be estimates.

Dedication

This book is dedicated to my daughter, Mia. I've loved watching you grow up and become the person you are today. I'm here for you to find your strength and footing in this world. You inspire me to do better...be better... and I love you always.

The house I build in this book is for Sydni. I only met you briefly, but your strength and grace in the face of immense adversity was beyond humbling, and you made a lifelong impact on me in the short time that you shared your story with me.

Photo credit: Eileen Fitzmaurice

Foreword

I first met Chris Schapdick at the bustling
New Jersey Tiny House Festival back in
2017. There, my partner, Christian, and
I were among thousands of attendees
who toured Chris's first tiny house on
wheels. Although the overall design was
familiar, from the moment we walked in
the door, we knew his home was special.
The way Chris brought the space to life
was spectacular. It was no surprise that
he ended up winning the Best Tiny House
award at the event.

Over the last several years, Christian
and I have toured hundreds of tiny homes
across North America as part of Tiny
House Expedition, our documentary
and community education project. The
diversity of tiny house designs we've seen
is mind-blowing; the quality of each build,
and reasons for building, vary greatly.
However, one commonality, especially
among DIYers, is that tiny homes act as
self-portraits of their owners. By that, I
mean they showcase all the best aspects of
the builder's personality and style. Even
slight imperfections add genuine character.

Overall, there's a special kind of intimacy between the
builder and the structure that is so enchanting. Of course, this
is in addition to the endless charm of a movable tiny home that
you can take almost anywhere. I can personally attest to that
addictive quality. In fact, Christian and I have traveled 55,000
miles with our DIY tiny house on wheels over the course of four
and a half years.

During our travels, we've had the great pleasure of touring
several of Chris's tiny house creations at festivals across the
East Coast. Each one is unique and full of personality. This is no
surprise, knowing how truly vivacious Chris is. Both he and his
homes on wheels always make me smile.

Perhaps what makes Chris's work so memorable is his
creative use of materials, as well as artistic, aesthetically pleasing
detailing. For instance, in his first tiny house, he used an antique
ship porthole as a window in the front door—an appealing and
inventive choice. But it also provided a practical use. And Chris's

exceptional designer chops aren't just for looks. He is a skilled
builder who fuses beauty with functionality throughout all his
tiny houses.

Best of all, for you and your reading pleasure, Chris is a
master at creating engaging and easy-to-follow how-tos for
beginners. What's more, like me, he is a total tiny house nerd
passionate about sharing the power of small spaces with the
world. If you read his first book, *The Joy of Tiny House Living*,
you know what I'm talking about. The man makes you fall in
love with living and building tiny.

Enjoy journeying into the wide world of tiny houses with
one exceptional human and learning how to build your own
unique masterpiece!

—Alexis Stephens
Tiny House Expedition cofounder, *Living Tiny Legally*
documentary series codirector,
webmaster of *TinyHouseBuild.com* & *TinyHousePlans.com*,
and YouTube channel creator, *www.youtube.com/
tinyhouseexpedition1*

Table of Contents

PART I:
Getting Started, Getting Inspired

PART II:
Building

Gallery

You've picked up this book because you're interested in building your own tiny house of some kind. This book will walk you step-by-step through building one particular model of tiny house: a small and versatile camper that is sometimes affectionately called a gypsy wagon. It's an accessible starting point for any tiny house enthusiast. The total build costs less than $5,000 and takes just one month of full-time labor. Here's a tour through the finished home and all its features, furnished and ready to roll.

FRONT VIEW: The sun will warm the home quickly, since it's such a small space.

RIGHT SIDE: The afternoon glow highlights the natural wood accents.

LEFT SIDE: Installing several side windows allows plenty of natural light in your tiny home.

BACK VIEW (HITCH SIDE): There's a window here for when the view is something better than a truck!

The small size of this camper makes it easy to haul around and maneuver even on tricky back roads.

Human for scale. Yep, that's me.

This nighttime glow is a nice sight to come home to.

A functional door ledge is a handy spot for temporary storage.

Cutouts under the eaves add interest.

The split front door design means it's easy to air out the interior.

Floral details and bubble windows make the camper look like more than a box on wheels.

This top-down view of the whole space from the bed (hitch side) gives you an idea of the entire interior.

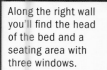

Along the right wall you'll find the head of the bed and a seating area with three windows.

The cushioned seating area includes a table for eating and working.

The bedside table, with its copper lamp, acts as a transition area between the seating area and the bed.

The natural slab of wood is an earthy touch that brings nature indoors.

Ceiling lights and a large hitch-side window provide ample lighting no matter the season.

This is a view to wake up to!

A cushion corner on the bed means ample seating for guests or just a change of position if you want to mix it up.

The left side of the camper holds the foot of the bed, shelving, and a kitchen cabinet area.

The kitchen includes a sink and wall space for hanging utensils.

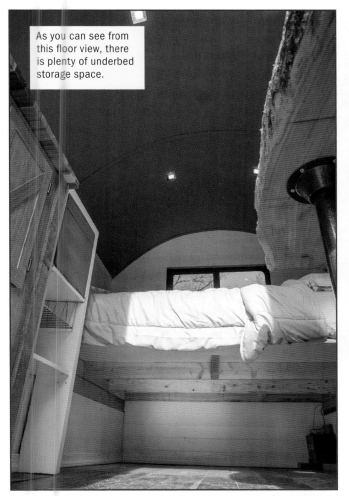

As you can see from this floor view, there is plenty of underbed storage space.

My personal stamp of completion.

When you're ready to retire, turn off the overhead lights and stick with the warm glow of the bedside lamp. Another tiny day done.

GETTING STARTED, GETTING INSPIRED

Before you dive right into building a tiny house, there are some basics to cover. My first book, *The Joy of Tiny House Living*, has a lot more detail about tiny house history, decisions about your tiny house design, and the philosophy behind tiny houses, but this chapter will give you the minimum you need to know. You'll also get the chance to hear from a couple who lives in the same kind of tiny house that this book teaches you to build.

Who and What Is This Book For?

In this book, we're going to build a tiny house on wheels together. It's a house that is a popular build that I make and sell with my company, Tiny Industrial. It's a little tiny house, not a big one, that's ultimately going to be your own custom, recreational, traveling tiny house. You don't have to follow the instructions all the way through to the end and build the exact type of tiny house that I show you here; you can branch off instead to build something that better suits your wants and needs. The step-by-step portion of this book (Part II) is divided into the shell and the customization. First you establish the shell: the four walls, the roof, the cutout for the door, the windows, and an empty interior that can become anything you want it to be. Then you make what you will of that interior. So, although I will show you how to take your blank slate and turn it into a livable tiny home on wheels, you don't need to take it to that level. Perhaps you just

need some guest space for your backyard. Maybe you want to build a space for your kids to hang out in. I've been considering making one of these for my teenage daughter so she can have a little bit of

You're going to build a house with this book. It will be a big, messy, impressive project. But it will be worth it.

After building this basic and structurally sound shell, you will be able to customize your tiny house however you like.

extra independence by just living in her own space and taking care of it, albeit in the relative safety and security of the backyard. The choice is yours. It could be a backyard office, a recording studio, a man cave, a she-shed, a place that you go to meditate. The possibilities are endless, and I will elaborate on some of the more creative uses throughout the book, but especially starting on page 124.

This is my second book on tiny houses. The first book, *The Joy of Tiny House Living*, is about contemplating your tiny house dreams and all that entails. It is less about doing and more about learning, imagining, and planning. It outlines all the considerations that go into either

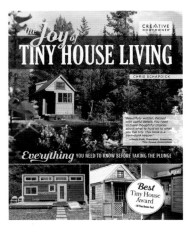

What This Book Does	... and What This Book Does Not Do
Teaches you the general step-by-step process of building a basic tiny house	Gives an exact architectural plan for you to follow inch by inch and cut by cut
Tells you which woodworking tools you'll need and why	Teaches you how to use all the woodworking tools you'll need
Gives you ideas for what to do and how to furnish your tiny house	Tells you how you must furnish your tiny house
Touches upon the many considerations you need to examine when deciding what to build	Details every single consideration you need to think about—that's what my first book, *The Joy of Tiny House Living*, is for!

purchasing or building your own tiny home—and I mean all of them, from lifestyle to toilets to insulation—but it is not a hands-on book. This book is designed to dive more into the hands-on aspect and actually walk you through building your own (small) tiny house. Think of it as a starter tiny home that you can create by using this book.

The detailed, nitty-gritty instructions and measurements that are in this book are unique to the particular type of trailer that I used. Not all the measurements, cuts, and builds that I do will be directly transferable to your project, because you may wind up with a differently sized or shaped trailer. For this reason, this is not going to be a book that says "cut this piece of wood to exactly 5 feet and 6 inches in length." Instead, it's going to give you transferable information that will allow you to independently adapt your own build as needed. If

protect you from the elements, is both thrilling and scary if you've never done it before. If you're going to embark on this journey, it is helpful if you already have some familiarity with basic building tools, something a little more advanced than just a hammer and a screwdriver. Your experience could be doing repairs to the deck on the back of your house. It could be putting together a bunk bed for your kids. Whatever the case is, some history with some form of construction is helpful—even having assembled numerous pieces of IKEA® furniture can qualify in this regard. I'm not going to go so far as to say it's a necessity for this book, though. Many people who built their own tiny homes did so while learning to use their tools for the very first time, and this could be true for you. But it adds a lot of time and stress and opens you up for mistakes. The

This headboard isn't an essential part of the build—it's a customization option—but by teaching you how I did it, I hope to give you the skills you need to figure out your own custom touches.

If you don't know what these tools are and how to use them, you'll need to learn before you build a tiny house. See page 34.

you do happen to get a very similar trailer to the one that I use for the build in this book, 95 percent of everything that I show you will be directly transferable to what you're doing.

The process of creating actual human shelter, something with four walls and a roof that will

focus of this book is not to teach you basic tool use, so make your own decisions about how to learn what you need to know before you get started.

If you're feeling a little nervous about embarking on such a big project, look for help. This could be in the form of family members who have some construction or DIY background. It could be by establishing contacts with folks online who are interested in supporting the tiny house community. The whole do-it-yourself community tends to be very supportive, and they embrace people who take that leap of faith and create things that they would never have thought they were capable of. I'm always happy to hear from people who are either looking to build their shelter or need some form of advice that I might have for them. I'm excited to impart that knowledge to people when and if I can, and this book is one way for me to do that.

Last but not least, I want to talk about self-confidence. Bringing a certain level of confidence to the project is essential. Without it, you're only going to doubt yourself and think that you can't do it. Let me take this opportunity to say, yes, you most likely can do this build. Yes, there are some physical capabilities you'll need in order to build any substantial structure. For instance, you will need to be able to lift 20 pounds (9kg) or more. However, unless there's some form of physical limitation that you may need assistance with, most people will be able to build something like this on their own. You have to start with the self-confidence of wanting to do it, and then the self-confidence boost that you will get from actually doing it is quite rewarding and not to be underestimated.

I hope that this gives you a clear picture of what I'm bringing to this book and what I'm asking you to

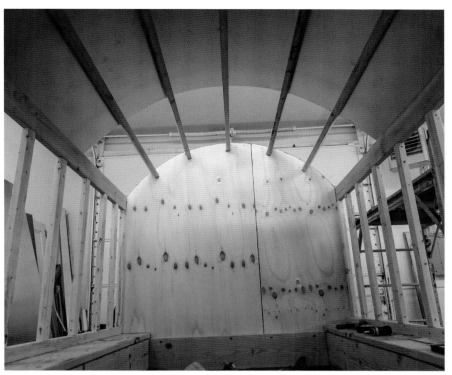

Someone—you—is going to have to lift and place roofing beams and aluminum roofing sheets. Remember, though, that you can always ask for help when you need it.

VIDEO LEARNING

I have put together a ton of video instruction to accompany Part II of this book. If, as you are following along, any of my descriptions or ways of doing things described in this book are not entirely clear, you can go to the video that corresponds with the specific part of the build for additional guidance and visuals. This will help you along and get you to the next step. Check out the videos at *www. youtube.com/c/tinyindustrial*.

bring to your build. Now, let's dive in and talk about tiny houses in general, their history, and why all of this is so relevant these days.

How I Ended Up in a Tiny House

Why should you trust me to teach you how to build a tiny house? In order to explain that, I need to tell you how I got started in the tiny house realm. My entry into the tiny living world didn't come from a background in the construction world. I was not busy building things; instead, I had a desk job that I didn't like. I realized that I wanted to do something different with my life, something that had less to do with sending e-mails back and forth all day long, analyzing spreadsheets, and creating PowerPoint presentations. I wanted to spend my time creating

something tangible instead of having a career based on nothing but zeros and ones. I had a need deep within me to do something substantive, to build with my hands.

That career crisis was coupled with my having a daughter who was growing up in a very suburban environment just outside of New York City. I witnessed how that conflicted with my own childhood experience. I grew up in Edmonton, Alberta, Canada. My childhood was filled with camping trips, fishing, skiing, snowshoeing, and

An aerial drone shot over my Catskills, NY, property. It was truly the retreat I was looking for with my daughter.

My daughter running around outside the same tiny house that I build in this book.

the land prices to be affordable, and I purchased a property there in 2013. This was right around the time that Jay Schafer's *The Small House Book* fell into my hands. Although my intention had always been to use my new land for weekend camping, I started to wonder about what kind of structure I could build on the property. The land had been affordable because it was zoned for recreational use only, meaning that no permanent structures could legally be built on the property. Realizing that I could have a house built on a trailer instead of a foundation got the wheels in my head turning.

At this time, the tiny house world was nascent. All the tiny house TV shows and media attention that came later hadn't happened yet. Tumbleweed Tiny House company out in California was one of the premier manufacturers and suppliers of all things tiny house at the time. So I bought some plans from them with the thought that I would build an entire tiny house myself. Unfortunately, the prospect was intimidating, and the land that I had purchased was a ninety-minute drive from where we lived, making quick construction sessions impossible.

Right around the same time, as if they were reading my mind, Tumbleweed released what they called an "Amish Barn Raiser." This was a shell of a house that they would build for you. In other words, they would do all the framing and sheathing, and you could opt to have them put the roof on, put windows in, and so on. The more you paid them to do, the less you had to do yourself. This appealed to me because it meant that I could effectively create my own space and vision of the tiny house while still having a significant part of the construction taken off my plate. Ultimately, this also saved me lots of time on what would have been a rather large structure to build as a beginner. (If you are curious about that first house I worked on, you can check it

all kinds of outdoor activities. I had the privilege to spend a lot of time in nature, and that left a big impression on me. Now a father myself, I was seeing my daughter not experiencing enough of that in her own life. Though we had been doing a fair amount of camping and other outdoor activities, it dawned on me that it would be ideal to have a piece of land that my daughter and I could travel to that would always be there and available for us to camp and spend time on—a dedicated retreat from urban life.

My research led me to a rural area northwest of New York City. It was suitably far enough away for

Hauling my first tiny house shell all the way from Colorado to New York.

out at *www.tinyhouseinthecountry.com*.) When you compare that structure to the scope of the one in this book, we're building something much smaller here, so the time frame, labor, and materials are not the same. That's preferable to biting off more than you can chew for your first build. What you want to do is get comfortable, and once you are, you can build more adventurous structures if you wish.

Although I started with a premade shell, it still became very much my own customized living space. My daughter and I needed a two-bedroom house, so I turned that house into a two-bedroom. There's a loft sleeping area for me, and then there's my daughter's separate bedroom in the back of the house. It still became a very personal project, even though the framing had been done for me. That is what I'd like to mimic in this book for you. We're going to slowly and carefully build the shell together, then see the possibilities for that shell and finish the

build together, while allowing you the flexibility to take your build in a different direction.

Once I completed that first tiny house, I took it to a tiny house show in New Jersey in 2017. It was a great experience. I had many people come through the house voicing their approval. What I had accomplished seemed to resonate with folks. At that show, I won the coveted "Best Tiny House in New Jersey" award. It was such a validation for me; I had done something that I had never expected to do, and I was being recognized for that work by experts. Building that first home pushed me beyond my comfort zone and indicated to me that perhaps I needed to shift my life and my priorities to do something more meaningful with my time on this planet. So I left my day job to do just that.

Now I write books like this one and build tiny houses as part of my company, Tiny Industrial. I enjoy being part of the broader community and

Hard at work customizing the shell.

helping others achieve what I did. Coupled with the books and the building, I also got my life coaching certification. Although I specialize in relationship coaching, I'm open to helping people work through what they want to do professionally. I'm sure that I'm not the only person who's ever pondered doing something like this with their life. I'm thrilled about what I've accomplished, and I want to impart that excitement

This is my first tiny house build next to the camper build in this book. The many differences are obvious!

This award helped me believe I could and should make a career out of tiny houses.

to others who are looking to change the trajectory of their lives. Think of this book as more than just a how-to book—think of it as something that can potentially have more significant ramifications in many areas of your life. This project will be good for your self-confidence, mindset, and sense of clarity for your life and dreams. Perhaps that's a lofty goal to get out of a how-to guide to building a tiny house. But hey, let's dream big and let's think bigger!

Dream as big as you want to.

A Snapshot of the Modern Tiny House Scene

Now that you've heard how I got into the tiny house lifestyle, let me tell you a little about the state of tiny houses and why they are they so popular today.

Tiny houses have been around forever, but our recent era of disposable income and general prosperity in the world has given rise to people building bigger and bigger houses. Not only are standard houses bigger but people fill them with more and more stuff, a symptom of rampant consumerism. We've gone so far in the direction of building and living in McMansions that people have started to realize several important things: (1) it's not making them happy, (2) they don't need to live in houses this large, and (3) there is something positive to be said about minimalism and downsizing.

People are starting to realize that they can live happier and more fulfilling lives in a fairy-tale cottage than they can in a McMansion.

I'm generalizing here, of course; everyone comes at tiny house living in a different way and with different and nuanced motivations. Some latch onto the financial angle, saying, "I'm spending all this money on housing. How can I spend less without discomfort or major sacrifice?" Some people come at it from an environmental place, saying, "This endless consumption, this growth of waste and excess in larger-space living, is not sustainable, and I want to do my part to live smaller and have a smaller carbon footprint." Young people coming out of college with lots of debt often look at living small and say, "This could be a really viable way for me to avoid further debt (like a mortgage) while still maintaining my independence." For all these reasons and more, interest in tiny homes has skyrocketed over the past decade, sprouting YouTube channels, books, construction companies, and more.

The specific reasons why people choose to go tiny are as diverse as the houses they go tiny in!

People often ask me, "Are tiny houses just a fad?" No, they are not a fad. Fidget spinners were a fad. Pokémon Go was a fad. We are witnessing a true shift in people's mindsets for a variety of reasons, and so we're seeing more people seeking alternative forms of housing.

This phenomenon has created a significant challenge to standard housing conventions. There are numerous and well-established housing, zoning, and planning norms that smaller, unconventional structures like tiny houses sometimes butt heads with. Although the process has been slow, over time more and more municipalities are allowing people to live in smaller structures. There is a massive need for affordable housing in the United States. Many municipalities don't have a good answer for housing shortages, so they're accepting accessory dwelling units (ADUs). An ADU is simply a small, secondary structure on a property that already has an actual house on it. This creates potentially affordable housing while not putting any additional infrastructure burden on the municipality in the form of sewer or electric provision—so it's a bit of a win-win for all involved.

I'm excited about the tiny house movement, and that's why I'm sharing this book with you. I hope

The increase in zoning laws for accessory dwelling units (ADUs) makes situating your tiny house more feasible.

that some of that excitement rubs off and this book helps you bridge that gap between just being curious about tiny houses to actually building your own four-walled space. Anyway, that's me on my soapbox about tiny houses and why they're so great. If you want a deeper dive into the hows and whys of tiny house living, my first book is a great place to start. It contains interviews with several full-time tiny house dwellers who share their personal stories as to why tiny house living was right for them, as well as more

detailed information on modern motivations for tiny house living, minimalism, and more.

The tiny house movement has grown by leaps and bounds in recent years, and you're taking your first steps to becoming a part of that movement.

Fundamentals

Before you pick up a hammer or buy yourself a trailer to accomplish Part II of this book, there are some important things I want to share with you. I want to go over safety essentials as well as the tools you'll need to execute the build in this book. Don't skip reading this section—make it a priority.

Safety

Goggles aren't geeky—they're essential.

First and foremost, I want you to work safely and be safe during your build. I don't want anyone to get injured in any way, shape, or form. Be very aware of your safety at all times. There are times during my build, photographed and filmed for this book, where I don't follow my own advice on the following (shame on me): wearing gloves whenever possible when it makes sense, wearing hearing protection

when dealing with loud noises, and wearing eye protection! Do not take my example literally if you ever see me not wearing safety glasses—that is a big mistake. Do as I say, not as I do: always wear the protection you need. Nothing—I repeat, **nothing**—is worth losing a finger or an eye over. And if there is something worth losing a finger or eye over, it's definitely not the pursuit of building a tiny house. Power tools make no distinction between cutting what they are supposed to be cutting and cutting what they are not supposed to be cutting. It is purely on you to ensure that what gets cut is wood, not your finger. To make sure you stay safe, adhere to the following four points:

- **Take your time.** This is not a sprint. You want to get to the finish line in one piece, not in first place.

- **Focus.** Give the process the full respect that it deserves. Everyone knows that being distracted isn't good when driving; well, it's also not good when working with power tools.

- **Protect yourself.** Wear gloves and eye protection. Wear a mask for particularly dusty situations. Read the warnings and instructions when working with chemicals. Do what you have to and what you can to minimize your exposure to the dangers posed by the materials and tools. Even something as small as getting a bad splinter is no fun, so take the easy precautions to avoid injury. More details about types and uses of safety equipment are on page 36.

- **Stay in your comfort zone.** This point deserves a more detailed explanation; read on.

Stay in Your Comfort Zone

Normally, I don't encourage people to stay in their personal and social comfort zones. After all, this whole book is, in a way, about getting out of your comfort zone, and doing something you've never done before. But when it comes to safety, I definitely want you to stick to your comfort zone. If it doesn't feel right, or if you are hesitant or reluctant in any way about doing any of the things outlined in this book, then don't do them. Bring in help. Ask for assistance (see page 34). Not doing these things could put you in danger. This could be anything from not feeling comfortable about lifting something heavy to using a particular kind of power tool. If you can't or don't want to do it, then don't.

Of course, your house won't get built if you're too afraid to touch any of your tools. You need to teach yourself to be comfortable and confident in handling your tools in whatever way works for you. If you have the option, I encourage you to attend a tiny house building workshop. These happen from time to time in various locations around the United States. Try to attend one to learn the basics about the proper use of tools and to arm yourself with the skills that will be relevant for this kind of build. If you can't find something specific to tiny houses, then look for something that has a more general construction theme. I have even seen the big-box hardware stores offering some limited classes on various construction topics. Another option might be to hire a contractor for a private lesson on whatever tools you may have purchased, borrowed, or rented to build with.

There is no one right path here; the right path is simply the one that makes you feel able to proceed and comfortable doing so. I have been building tiny houses for years now, and (knock on wood) I have never injured myself in any significant way. Some

Stay grounded and stay in your comfort zone. Don't worry about a bit of mud, as long as you are confident about what you're doing.

of that is luck, but the much bigger component is taking the necessary care and being confident in my abilities to tackle a given task. Explore the boundaries of your comfort zone with skydiving, public speaking, etc., but not with power tools and things that can irreparably harm you.

Assistance

Rome was neither built in a day nor built by one person. Although I'm content to build these tiny houses on my own, that doesn't mean that *you* have to. In fact, quite the opposite. I encourage you to get as many people involved as you possibly can (within reason). Not only does that help with the whole momentum of the project, but it's also a great way for you to spend time with folks, teach them about tiny houses, and get the help you need, all at the same time. Help can come in many forms: finances, expertise, and a simple helping hand where four hands are better than two. Focus on what you believe you need most and seek out folks with those skills. Who do you know that could be useful for a project of this kind? Who in your extended family would be interested in this sort of thing? Sometimes it's not immediately clear, and you might be surprised at who and what you can leverage. Buy them a beer. Pick their brain. Barter. Help is out there, so use it.

Bringing others on board not only helps you, but it can also bring additional perspective to the project.

Tools

Contrary to popular belief, you don't need a lot of tools to create what we're building here. There is a minimum number of tools that you'll need, and then every tool beyond that will make your work either easier or more precise. Don't think that you have to spend $1,000 on all sorts of things. It is even possible to build a tiny house with all hand tools, and people have done it. Power tools are a great thing, though, and I highly encourage their use (see page 35 for more info on power tools). Just understand that certain tools will make the process easier. You may or may not have access to those tools, and you may or may not want to use them, borrow them, or rent them. Decide what works for you.

The pictures in this chapter are of my well-used tools. They are nothing fancy, but they work just fine, and I have built multiple houses with them. You may find yourself gravitating toward other tools as you work and gain more experience, but these are a great starting point.

Get ready to go to the hardware store and buy some supplies. You're pretty darn close to starting to build your own tiny house on wheels.

Connected/Wired Tools versus Battery-Operated Tools

Tools broadly fall into one of two categories: hand tools and power tools. Power tools, in general, are a bit more expensive than hand tools, but unless you have some personal reason to use only hand tools, power tools will make your life a whole lot more comfortable, and I recommend spending the money on them.

When I was growing up, there were power tools that plugged into the wall, but there were really no such things as battery-operated tools. For that reason, I gravitated to standard 110V connected power tools. There is nothing inherently wrong with that approach today. What has happened over the last 20 years or so, though, is a shift to battery-powered tools. These have come down a lot in cost, and you are not sacrificing anything in regard to performance anymore. Batteries are more efficient and less expensive, and all this has led to a major shift in the power tool industry. I'm a fairly recent adoptee of this technology, but I can see that the benefits are vast. There are many advantages of using battery-powered tools:

- They eliminate the need to have a power supply close to where you are working. You can take your tools and a bunch of batteries and do work in the middle of the woods. Your ability to work is only limited to your battery capacity.
- You don't have to worry about cords getting in the way, either. It is such a simple thing, but it can make all the difference for some people in terms of ease of use and comfort.

Sounds great, right? The benefits tend to outweigh the downsides. But of course, there are a few downsides.

- Battery-powered tools tend to be more expensive.
- Once you decide on a brand of battery-powered tools, you are effectively locked into that brand, since the batteries are not compatible with other manufacturers' tools.
- If your batteries run out of power and you can't recharge them, you can't work anymore.
- There will always be some tools that you won't be able to get a battery-operated version of, such as a table saw, miter saw, and air compressor.

Make the tool choices that make sense to you, your budget, and your style of work.

A wired screwdriver and a battery-operated screwdriver. Each has its pros and cons.

The battery is removed from the base to be recharged; if you have more than one battery, you can swap the dead one out for a fresh one while it recharges.

Safety Equipment

Nothing worth building is worth injuring yourself for. Since this is a hands-on building book, I am going to emphasize safety again and again. Your eyes, ears, and fingers are all susceptible to damage, as well as the rest of your body. It's more than just a good idea to do what you can to protect them. Although protection is no guarantee that you won't get hurt, it does reduce risk tremendously.

Safety goggles or glasses and gloves are great to just get used to wearing when you are working.

Gloves, goggles, and earmuffs: the trifecta of protection. Not pictured: a dust mask to protect your lungs.

Even something as simple as a splinter can have a negative impact on your work. This is especially true if you are dealing with pressure-treated lumber (the chemicals in the wood lead to a very painful reaction). Hearing protection in the form of earmuffs or earplugs is a good idea when you are using tools like an impact driver, router, table saw, or miter saw. They are pretty loud, and over time they will negatively impact your hearing. Working with these tools and going to lots of rock concerts in the 1980s have done their part to contribute to some hearing loss for me. It's pretty easily avoidable, though, so either do something to protect your hearing or get used to having that steady, high-pitched ringing in your ears forever, like I do. You can pick up these three items (safety goggles, gloves, and hearing protection) for about $75 total.

There are also certain parts of the build that are particularly dusty, so it's not a bad idea to have some sort of filtration safety mask for those times. Depending on how susceptible you are to the effects of dust inhalation, you may want to consider investing more or less in this. You can go super cheap with simple, disposable masks for a couple bucks a pop, or more expensive and effective valved filtration masks that cost $20 to $40. If you find that wearing the mask all the time is too restrictive, don't worry about leaving it off—you'll know when you are creating lots of dust, so just wear it during those times. And, of course, always use it if working with fiberglass, other forms of insulation, or certain chemical substances.

Tools: The Bare Minimum

So, what are the tools that you will absolutely need for tiny house construction?

- **Circular saw:** because you'll need to cut things
- **Power drill with bits and attachments:** because you'll need to attach things together
- **Miscellaneous:** straight edges, pencils, a level, a hammer, screws, nails, etc.

That's it! With these two power tools and a few supplementary items, you can build a tiny house. I don't recommend that you proceed with just these two tools, but my point is that there is no need for tons of expensive equipment. You can buy these two power tools for under $100 each.

Tools: Well Worth It

Let me add some other tools that make the job much more manageable, quicker, and more accurate. I consider the tools in this section to be highly recommended additions to your tool arsenal. These tools combined will cost you between $500 and $1,000, depending what quality grade (i.e., brand) you go with. With the exception of the jigsaw ($30) and the wrenches and ratchets ($30–$70), the other items all run between $100 and $150. Remember, you can always buy some of these used or you can borrow them to save money.

Miter saw: These are great to make accurate right-angle cuts. They also can cut at angles other than 90 degrees (typically up to 45 degrees). Since tiny houses are often constructed with 2x4s (50x100mm) for the framing, this tool is invaluable for making numerous and exacting cuts to specific lengths. Can you frame a house without a miter saw? Sure you can, but I wouldn't want to.

Circular saw. This is useful for cutting things in a reasonably straight, unprecise sort of way.

Power drill. My old one finally died, and this one is a relatively new addition to my stockpile of tools.

Miter saw. This is an inexpensive one, but it gets the job done.

Cordless impact driver:
Have you ever tried to screw in a 3" (7.5cm) screw by hand? In case you haven't, I can tell you: it's not fun. Now imagine having to screw in a couple hundred screws like this. This is where the cordless impact driver comes in. It is an electric, motorized screwdriver on steroids. It's a recent addition to my toolkit, but I wouldn't want to do without one of these anymore; I screw all my framing together with this tool. Screws create stronger bonds than nails and are therefore preferable. You can use a good power drill to drive screws as well, which is what I used to do, but a cordless impact driver is way more convenient, since it comes in a small, lightweight format and is excellent for powering in any number of different fasteners. The impact part of this tool also differs from a regular power drill in that it utilizes a hammering mechanism to spin the fasteners into place.

Jigsaw: You will need to make rounded cuts or lop off corners of things. The circular saw is not going to do that for you; it's too big and cumbersome. Enter the jigsaw. This works great on lots of different materials, and you can swap the blades for whatever your current cutting task requires. An inexpensive corded jigsaw will do.

Cordless (battery-powered) impact driver. It's small and versatile, yet also very powerful at driving screws.

Jigsaw. One of these gives you some more precision in cutting and is very good at cutting curves and making rounded cuts.

Air compressor. Compresses air, which is then used to power various things you can hook up to it.

The gauges on the air compressor show you how much pressure is in the tank and how much you are delivering to whatever you have hooked up to it. You can dial the pressure up or down based on the needs of the device.

Air compressor and nail guns: I use this combo for interior work, mostly. The compressor fills an air chamber with pressurized air, which then can be used to power various devices. The main thing I use a compressor for is to use a finishing nailer to shoot very fine and thin (headless) nails. These are great for fastening pieces of trim or interior paneling. On my first tiny house build, I also used a framing nailer to secure the cedar siding to my house. This is a much bigger gun than the finishing nailer, and it shoots rather large nails efficiently, quickly, and repeatedly. You can even get an attachment for your compressor to fill your car tires; it mimics the machine at the gas station that puts air in your tires. This can come in handy and will save you the occasional dollar!

Framing nailer. This is the heavy-duty version of the finishing nailer. It shoots huge nails into things you want to attach together.

Finishing nailer. Use this for attaching interior trim in such a way that you can barely see the nails. Fast and efficient, it beats gluing stuff on the walls.

Wrenches and ratchets: Early in the build, you will be mounting the beginnings of the tiny house structure to the frame of the trailer. This is the one point where we will be working with bolts instead of screws. It is also the point where you will need to tighten some nuts onto those bolts. To do so, you will need either wrenches or ratchets. What's the difference? A wrench is typically a dedicated tool that pertains to a specific size of bolt head or nut (as compared to pliers or vise grips, which don't have dedicated sizing). They are sold in sets for around $30. A ratchet is paired with sockets. Those sockets come in various sizes. You pair the ratchet with the socket you need, and the ratchet is an extension to the sockets that allows you to tighten or loosen a nut or bolt. They come in various sizes, with the larger ratchets giving you more leverage than the smaller ones. Pricing will vary a lot based on the number of sockets and the quality of the product; expect to pay about $70 for a pretty good set. The other advantage to a ratchet is that it allows you to stay connected to what you are loosening or tightening because there is an internal mechanism that only allows the socket to be turned forward or backward (selectively); this makes for a quicker and easier process. With a standard wrench, you have to disconnect and reconnect to whatever you are loosening or tightening after each motion.

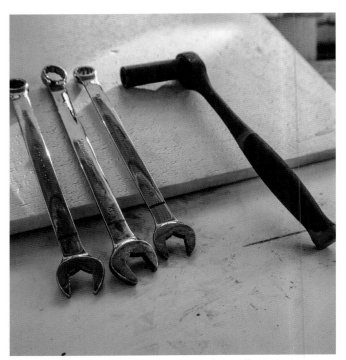

Wrenches and ratchets are fairly ubiquitous items; if you don't own them, odds are that you know someone who does.

These come in two broad flavors: metric (sized in millimeters) and SAE (Society of Automotive Engineers) (sized in inches). The two kinds have a certain level of cross-compatibility, so don't get too hung up on having one or the other.

Tools: Handy Extras

There are a few more tools that I love having on hand. You can expect to spend about $350 total on these four tools.

Oscillating multi-tool: This thing is excellent for achieving those nearly impossible cuts. It works by essentially vibrating a blade back and forth. That blade is typically a relatively narrow one. When you have to trim something off a piece that has already been installed, this is a lifesaver. It provides small, precise cuts that no other power tool can make in that situation.

Random orbital electric sander: Sanding with sandpaper is okay once in a while. You can use a file for some other jobs. But for larger-scale smoothing, an orbital sander is ideal. You can stick various grits of sandpaper onto it, and the vibrating action takes most of the elbow grease out of the equation. I reach for this tool frequently during construction.

Oscillating multi-tool. You attach one of the various kinds of blades to the front of this and it vibrate-cuts its way through things. It's great for getting you out of a tough spot during a build.

The multi-tool getting ready to do what it does best in its natural construction environment.

Electric sander. This will save you a lot of elbow grease.

The sander is great for smoothing out a broad wood surface like this. Progressively finer grits of sandpaper on the sander lead to a buttery smooth finish.

Table saw: You can make long cuts with a circular saw and with a jigsaw, but getting those cuts perfectly straight is not possible. A table saw allows you to make perfect long cuts, since it's designed to keep the blade straight as you run a piece of wood through it. The fence on the top of the table saw gets locked into place at a specific distance from the blade. That distance determines the width of the cut. Whatever you push across the top of the table saw is cut precisely to that width. Safety should always be a top concern, but this is especially true with a table saw—it's one of the more dangerous tools I've included in this section. This is mostly because you are pushing an item into a cutting blade. Don't slip. Wear eye protection (always). Stay clear of the blade. For smaller, narrower cuts, there is a device called a push stick that you can use to push the object through the blade. It's an extension of your hand, with the difference being that if the push stick gets in the blade, it's no big deal. If you choose not to use a push stick, be ready to call for an ambulance with your undamaged hand.

Table saw. Make sure you have one of these when you absolutely need to cut in a straight line.

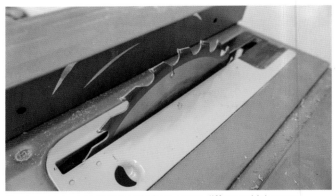

You can raise and lower the blade to cut to different thicknesses.

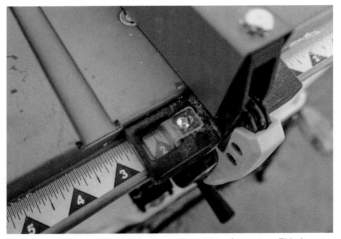

The table saw fence is where you set the width of your cut. This is set for 2" (5cm). You can see it in the small window.

This is the push stick. Alternatively, you can use a scrap of wood to push things through the blade. Either way, don't let your hands get near the blade. The blade will always win.

Router: This is the latest entry into my personal toolbox. A router is a direct-drive tool that spins interchangeable cutting attachments to create shapes and cuts. The depth of the cut can be adjusted. This thing is phenomenal for doing window and door cutouts in plywood. It's also great for cabinetry. Much like a drill, there are router bits that you can purchase that achieve certain purposes. A drill simply drills differently sized holes based on what drill bit you are using. A router is a different beast in that the bits do different things. One bit might put a fancy scalloped edge on a piece of wood. When a wood counter has that nice, curved edge, it was likely created with a router. The bit that is my main go-to is one that is a cylindrical cutter with a ball bearing at the very top. What that allows for is cutting along predefined cutouts, so I like using it for cutting door and window openings. If you have a window framed out in a wall and then you cover that framing with plywood, you can really put this to good use.

I have two routers: a large ($80) one with more power, and a small ($40) one intended for jobs that require a bit more finesse.

This is the small ball bearing that keeps the blade on track to cut out what you want it to.

Here the cutting bit has been recessed deeper into the tool, implying that you are cutting into thinner material.

Drill a quick hole into that plywood and insert this router bit. The bit is designed to cut up to the edge of the frame and no further. As you proceed around the perimeter of the frame, it makes a beautiful, clean cut all around, since the ball-bearing part of the bit traces its way around the perimeter of the framed-out part behind the plywood being cut.

Here is a smaller router with a cutting bit that does not have the ball bearing. This one will simply do a plunge cut into whatever material you guide it into.

Tools: Miscellaneous Consumables and Implements

In a book like this, it's impossible for me to talk about and describe every single thing that you may possibly need along the way. It's also likely counterintuitive to do so. Just know that there will be a number of basic items that will make building easier, and I consider these things to be standard equipment in anyone's toolbox. These items include measuring tapes, pliers, hammers, screwdrivers, carpenter squares, box cutters, clamps, saw horses, utility knives, caulking, and so on.

You will use these on an as-needed basis; many of them you'll only use once, and they are not going to break the bank. In fact, you may already have a few of these things already. Try to borrow what you can from friends, family, or coworkers. These are the basics of any work that you do, whether you are building a birdhouse or an actual house. All of these items together should cost no more than $100.

Clamps, pencils, hammer, utility knives, etc.: you'll know when you need them. These are a kind of baseline minimum when you are building anything.

What It's Like to Live in the Tiny House

Can you imagine living here?

Emily and Dan Moore are full-time gypsy wagon dwellers who live in the very same tiny house that you'll learn to build in this book. Of course, as with any tiny house, it has its own customizations, personality, and story. I sat down with Emily and Dan to get their story and to give you a glimpse of what it could be like to live in your build. Check out the photos to see how their home came together, the items they added and what they went without, and read their inspiring story.

Emily and Dan, who have been married for twenty-four years, were first introduced to the world of tiny houses through TV shows. Emily fell in love with several shows dedicated to tiny houses, which drove her to do more research, purchase a book on the topic, attend a workshop, and then come home one day and inform her husband that she was going to build a tiny house. Dan was uninterested at first, but after the pair attended a tiny house festival together, he was converted, and they started working on a plan. It was around this time, September 2017, when they met me at a Tennessee tiny house festival.

FIND OUT MORE

For more details on the nitty-gritty of how Emily and Dan equipped their home with a shower, sink, and toilet, see pages 159–165!

The door of Emily and Dan's full-time residence, lovingly dubbed "My Crow House."

"Chris and I spent many hours talking back and forth about the structure. He had some excellent ideas, which helped me and Emily on our build," said Dan. "It looks similar to Chris's, and it turned out very nice. Chris is a very talented young man." (Thanks for the compliment, Dan!)

Before they got started on the build, the couple, self-described as "empty nesters," began giving away possessions to their children or anyone who would take things. "I saw Dan give away his 60" (152cm) TV and his grill; he also sold his truck. When I saw him doing these things, I knew we were truly on the same page," said Emily. They finally bought their trailer in October 2018 and started building in February 2019. In the end, it took the pair about six months to build their beloved "My Crow House," as they named it, and they have been living in the house full time since the summer of 2019.

The home is constructed on a 5' x 10' (152.4 x 304.8cm) trailer. The windows are roadside finds that cost the couple exactly $0. The small gray box up front is the power inlet for the house.

The air conditioning and heating are provided by this single window-style standard unit. In a small space, any size air conditioner will be sufficient to cool the place down. This is a 6000 BTU unit that also has the advantage of being a heater. That way, it checks two boxes and negates the need for an additional heating unit.

This trailer has a standard leveling jack on the hitch. Emily and Dan also retrofitted brakes onto the trailer so that their tow vehicle does not have to bear the entire burden for slowing their house down when rolling down the road.

"It has honestly been one great big adventure, because you're waking up in your home every day, and you might be in a different spot, but you know you're at home, and you have all your belongings with you," said Dan. "It's just awesome." Emily added, "Home is where you park it."

The seeds for the tiny house were planted in Emily long before she first came across the tiny house TV shows that would ultimately change their lives. As a child, she was used to seeing excess, in the form of a china cabinet full of dishes that were never used, or suitcases of clothing that were never

The fold-down shelf on the side of the house doubles as an outdoor kitchen, housing Emily and Dan's propane camping stove with room to spare. Such a small interior space encourages cooking outdoors.

worn, but these excesses never made sense to her. As she got older, she said, "I found that the fewer things I had, the happier, and more at peace, I felt within myself. I wasn't keeping up with taking care of all this crap or worried about having crap." Fewer possessions took up less mental space and energy, allowing her to feel free to do more hiking, to go to the beach, and, ultimately, to take her house with her when she did. "Less stuff turned into having more experiences for us," she explained. This extends to gift giving, too; now, the pair like to give and receive experiences, like a trip to a winery, rather than something that would weigh down a trailer.

Camping stoves come in various sizes and styles. This Coleman utilizes very easy-to-obtain 16-ounce (0.45kg) propane cylinders (mounted on the right side). The stove also features a grill top. Whether cooking a full meal or simply boiling a pot of water for making coffee, this stove is always ready.

The shelf support chain doubles as a great paper towel holder. There is a small prep area next to the cooker. This configuration works for Emily and Dan, but the shelf could be made bigger or smaller according to individual needs.

Their home is built on a 5' (152.4cm) wide by 10' (304.8cm) long trailer. All told, it weighs about 2,800 pounds (1,270kg), which makes it possible to tow it with a 2013 Volkswagen Tiguan. "Our goal was to be lightweight so that we could make it as mobile as possible. This thing was built with love, passion, and compromise," said Emily.

Their kids, who are in their twenties, love it, too. Dan explained, "They'll say, 'Hey, we want to borrow your house to take it somewhere.' And I'll reply, 'Okay, we'll come house sit for you, and you can take our house and go on an adventure!'" It's a great system that works for the whole family.

Organization in a small space is key. Emily keeps her toiletries in a cloth organizer that she can take outside with her. The space where the cooktop resides also transforms into the space where the outdoor shower is located. The showerhead connects to the interior kitchen sink when in use.

Just because a space is small doesn't mean that you can't decorate a bit. Swatting flies in style and displaying maps on such a mobile home foster a uniqueness and personality that is specific to Emily and Dan. It all underscores the creation of a deeply personal space and home for the two of them.

Chalkboard paint is a fun material. When not leaving love notes for one another on this board, Emily and Dan affectionately display the name they have given their home.

Dan and Emily aren't worried about where they'll get money to put gas in the tank. For one thing, they own the house outright, so they aren't trapped in a mortgage. Emily works as a traveling nurse, so she can choose her assignments by region and move there—home in tow—for the duration of the contract. As for Dan? "Who knows what Dan will do. Dan is a man of many talents," said Emily.

One of the many questions Emily and Dan were asked repeatedly, even within the first few months of living in their home, was "Why would you go through all the trouble to build something like this when you could just buy a small manufactured camper?" Dan's answer was simple: "A camper is not personal to what you like, your vision. You build a

The beautiful brown, weathered appearance of the wood on the exterior of this house was achieved using the ancient Japanese wood preservation technique known as *shou sugi ban*. Wood is scorched and then brushed to create this wonderful look.

To the left of the door is the doorbell and a shoe basket. It's easier to keep the interior clean if shoes stay outside. The step down from the interior to the ground outside provides a great place to sit to put on and take off your shoes.

The roof overhang offers a dry spot outside when it's raining. It's also a nice visual element beyond its practical role. Hooks allow Emily and Dan to attach hanging plants (when not en route) to further enhance the exterior.

When traveling, there isn't always power available to run interior appliances. For such occasions, Emily and Dan utilize a standard cooler (tucked under the right corner of the house). They can still enjoy healthy meals on the road and sample local specialties while saving money by not having to eat out.

When you live in a 50-square-foot (4.6-square-meter) house, there is no shortage of curiosity, and you may need to be prepared to tell your story and give tours. Emily and Dan are great ambassadors of tiny living and are always happy to explain all the positive impacts that this lifestyle has had for them.

tiny house around *you*." Emily noted that campers are cookie cutter, and that is fine for some people, and she doesn't criticize them for their choice, but it wasn't her and Dan's goal; they wanted a true and permanent home, not something to use just a few times a year. They are connected to their home to an even deeper degree than most people are to their traditional homes, as well, due to the simple, practical fact that they built it themselves. "We know every screw; we picked out every board that's in here. Every board in this house has been touched by either one of us or both of us. And we know how it is all put together," said Emily. "If there is ever any issue, we know how to deal with it."

So far they haven't had to deal with any serious issues, and they haven't even had to deal with the one "issue" many people mention when talking to them about their home: "I could never live in anything this small." At just 50 square feet

(4.6 square meters), it's true that the couple is low on real estate. But that's simply not a problem for them. They use their home to sleep, eat, sit and talk, and more, but they spend a lot of time outside. "You look out the door, there's a whole front yard, no matter where you are," said Dan. Even when they do spend longer amounts of time inside, they don't mind. "Everyone that walks in here talks about how cozy it is," said Emily. Visitors can also literally feel the love coming from the house, as Dan experienced when two people came by and told him as much. "That made me feel great. That's what it's all about," he said.

Doing what Emily and Dan are doing, changing their lives and condensing them physically into a smaller space, isn't a one-time, dramatic makeover, but rather a learning process, and it's not at all limited to the physical. The transformation has changed how Emily sees the world and herself. She stopped blow-drying, straightening, and coloring her hair, saving her time, effort, and money. "I'm more accepting of who I am as a person and what I look like," she explained. "I'm done with trying to fit into some societal norm; I've just allowed myself to be me, and I have found

There are not a lot of homes where you can see the entire interior just by looking in the door. What this house lacks in size it makes up for in style and the depth of thought that invariably has to go into all elements in a structure this small.

The underbed area comprises the bulk of the storage available to Emily and Dan. On the right is a rod to hang clothes under the bed. Summer and winter wardrobes and other things that don't need to be accessed daily reside deeper under the bed platform. Emily and Dan utilize a "dry toilet," which is the bucket-type object to the left. Read more about toilet types on page 159.

that to be the most freeing thing. This house is just an extension of that." Emily has also been making an effort to push herself past her fears, by doing things like going camping by herself and learning to tow the house herself. Since tomorrow is never promised, she says, she wants to be ready for anything.

This is the essential core of one piece of advice that the pair would give anyone interested in getting their own tiny house project off the ground. "Try your best to get over your fears, and do what you want to feel liberated and free," Dan stated. "Have the courage every day to walk toward that goal," said Emily. As a nurse, she has direct experience holding people's hands at the ends of their lives, spending brief but important moments with them and trying to help them through whatever they are experiencing. All three of us, while talking, agreed that at the end of their

The kitchen area is for both food prep and storing and organizing all of Emily and Dan's cooking utensils. There is a sink and faucet, but no integrated stove or cooktop. The couple does the bulk of their cooking outside. Conveniently, with the window open, they have easy access between the exterior propane cooker and any things they might need from the inside.

Clutter is easy to create in any home. When you have a home this small, you have to be extra-vigilant. Wall-mounted storage helps to tame the countertop area and provides a cool-looking industrial accent as well.

In a well-organized tiny house, everything has its place. If you don't have a specific place to store it, you have to really consider if it's worth having in the first place. A tiny space will also glaringly show you what you don't use and therefore don't need. Emily and Dan still regularly get rid of things for this reason, even though they have already downsized their life substantially.

The "living room" of Emily and Dan's tiny house. Relax. Stare out the window. Curl up with a good book. When you do it right, tiny equals cozy.

A bedside table or a storage shelf? This is both. (The large stuffed animal is optional.)

lives (and before), people mostly regret the things that they didn't do. "We're all just one life event away from being a different person," Emily reflected. "If there's something that you want to do, push past your reservations and do it." The couple's main regret, if you want to call it that, is simply that they waited so long to go tiny in the first place.

But now they have made the leap, and they are taking advantage of a world with more and more freedoms in it to be who they want to be. It was clear to me from the moment I met them that they were really passionate about their tiny house goals. It warmed my heart to sit in their lovely home and talk about their journey with them. As Dan pointed out, "The greatest thing is that we've been around so many people who have inspired us on this journey. It's just incredible." They inspire me as much as I inspired them, and I hope that their story inspires you.

PART II

BUILDING

It's what you've been waiting for: building your tiny house. My goal in this part of the book is to also build your self-confidence in the beginning stages, while we're constructing the same thing (the shell). Then I'll send you on your way with newly acquired skills and confidence to customize your own structure. We'll also examine your options for a kitchen and bathroom in such a tiny space.

Step-by-Step Building the Shell

Okay, enough of all this theoretical stuff—let's build something! That's why you bought this book, right?

We're going to start by building a shell. What exactly is a shell? Let's use the analogy of painters. They start with a blank canvas, and then they create their work of art on that canvas. When we talk about creating the shell of a tiny house, we're talking about creating the canvas.

Your shell will include four walls and a roof mounted to a trailer. It will serve as the starting point for building anything you want. Much like a painter can turn a blank canvas into any painting, the same holds true for the shell. It can be turned into an office, a yoga studio, a recording studio, or a camper, as we'll be doing later on in this book. The shell is the fundamental thing that turns a trailer and a pile of wood into a tiny dwelling on wheels.

Now, I mentioned all of the following earlier in the book, but it all bears repeating. You're likely not going to have the same trailer that I build here. You may not have access to the same tools that I use. You may not have access to similar pieces of wood that I use. Plus, specific nuances with your trailer may

determine different lengths and thicknesses and structural requirements and so forth. Don't look at these images and descriptions and say, "Oh, mine isn't lining up exactly like that!" or "I'm doing this, and it's not turning out that way." Instead, look at it more as a general process, a step-by-step guide to tackling a building project that may seem daunting at first, but, when broken down, reveals itself to be achievable.

Although the dimensions, sizes, and materials that you use may be different than mine, the goals of what you are trying to accomplish are the same. I'll always describe the end goal as we're going. In many cases, the same or similar thing can be achieved in many different ways, so what I show in this book is just one way to do it. It might not even necessarily be the best way to do it, but it's the way that I do it. So take the instructions with a grain of salt. Focus more on the concepts and the steps to get from A to B rather than attempting to follow everything like an exact recipe. I'm here to teach you the process that you can use to build your own custom home. Here we go!

Frequently Used Lumber Sizes			
Nominal size (common name) in inches	Actual size in inches	Nominal size (common name) in metric	Actual size in metric
2x3	1½" x 2½"	50x75mm	38 x 64mm
2x4	1½" x 3½"	50x100	38 x 89mm
2x6	1½" x 5½"	50x150	38 x 140mm
2x12	1½" x 11¼"	50x300	38 x 286mm

Shell Build Breakdown

Section	Subsection	Materials (main)	Cost Estimate	Tools (main)	Time Estimate
Trailer Selection		N/A	$1,250	N/A	2 hours
Trailer Leveling		N/A	$40	Jack stands, level	1 hour
Initial Trailer Work	Closing in the Sides	2x12s, slats/shims, paint, stain	$100	Clamps, saw, paint supplies	6 hours
	Creating Bump-outs	2x12s, paint, stain	$100	Clamps, saw, paint supplies	5 hours
Front and Back Walls		Four 4' x 8' (121.9 x 243.8cm), ¾" (1.9cm) sheets of plywood, paint, sealant	$250	Jigsaw, carpenter square, measuring tape	10 hours
Mounting Everything Thus Far to the Trailer		2x4s, carriage bolts, silicone, adhesive	$35	Wrench, clamps	4 hours
Doorway		2x4s, adhesive, screws	$25	Router, impact driver	4 hours
Roofing Beams		12' (365.8cm) 2x4s (5x), 12' (365.8cm) 2x6s (2x)	$75	Hammer, miter saw	3 hours
Side Walls		8' (243.8cm) 2x3s (10x)	$50	Jigsaw, miter saw	8 hours
Roof Dry Fit		4' x 8' (121.9 x 243.8cm) sheets of aluminum (3x)	$250	N/A	3 hours
Front Window		Front window, 2x3s, 2x4s, glue, screws	$150	Jigsaw, impact driver	4 hours
Electrical	Installation	Pass-through cable, RV panel, battery, outlets, wire	$350	Wire cutter/stripper, drill	12 hours
	Lighting	12V LED lights, switch	$50	Wire cutter/stripper, drill, circle cutter	4 hours
Closing up the Side Walls and Adding Side Windows	Side Walls	½" (1.3cm) 4' x 8' (121.9 x 243.8cm) sheets of plywood (3x), paint, sealant, screws, silicone, adhesive	$150	Impact driver, paint supplies	6 hours
	Side Wall Windows	12" x 12" (30.5 x 30.5cm) windows (6x), 2x3s, cedar trim, silicone, screws	$250	Jigsaw, impact driver, table saw, air tool brad nailer	5 hours
Attaching the Roof		Adhesive, marker, silicone, screws	$50	Impact driver	7 hours
Trailer Floor	Creating a Vapor Barrier	Moisture barrier, tape, underlayment foam	$100	Knife	4 hours
	Finishing the Floor	Engineered wood or laminate flooring	$125	Miter saw	6 hours
Door		Plywood, pine planks, door hardware, paint (optional)	$150	Table saw, impact driver, paint supplies (optional)	8 hours
Interior Finishing	Insulation	Foam board, rock wool	$200	Knife	10 hours
	Finishing the Walls and Ceiling	Tongue-and-groove ¼" (0.6cm) pine planks, thin 4' x 8' (121.9 x 243.8cm) plywood for ceiling (3x)	$250	Jigsaw, miter saw, air tool brad nailer	8 hours
TOTAL			$4,000		120 hours

NOTE: Cost of tools not included in pricing estimates. These are rough estimates; your timing and cost of materials may vary.

Trailer Selection

Let's start by talking about the trailer. For this build, you should look for specific characteristics in the trailer that will make it ideal for what it will become.

1. Shown here is a 5' wide x 10' long (152.4 x 304.8cm) utility trailer. This is a trailer that you'll see landscapers and ATV owners use to haul their equipment.

2. This particular type of trailer has a pressure-treated wood deck. This is ideal because the flooring, or the base floor, is already done for you before you even get started. You'll see other trailers that have mesh decks, which is the most common alternative to pressure-treated wood. If you get a mesh deck, then you'll have to do some floor installation work.

3. This trailer also has a rail that runs around the outer edge of it. It is roughly about 1' (30.5cm) off the pressure-treated deck, and it will be essential to the construction. Find a trailer that has this railing. Mine does not have the rail in the back (non-hitch end), since there is typically a gate that folds down to form a ramp.

4. Another characteristic of the rail here is that it has a flat top. Basically, that rail structure is made out of angle iron, which is just a piece of steel that has been bent at a 90-degree angle, making it incredibly strong.

5. We're working with a steel utility trailer with a pressure-treated deck and an angle iron rail. If you can't find a trailer with the angle iron, your next best bet is a tube top trailer. By "tube," I mean a square tube, not a round tube. Round tubes are also out there, but they will make this build nearly impossible. This photo shows a great example of a trailer NOT to use: it has round tube, and it also has a mesh bottom, meaning you'll have to install some form of sub-flooring base.

Steel utility trailers with a pressure-treated deck and an angle iron rail, like other trailers, come in different sizes. I have seen them in 5' x 8' (152.4 x 243.8cm), 5' x 10' (152.4 x 304.8cm), and 6½' x 10' (198.1 x 304.8cm). The one I'm using happens to be a 5' x 10' (152.4 x 304.8cm). These dimensions are the deck sizes, not the overall dimensions of the trailer. Overall dimensions are going to be bigger due to the wheel wells and the hitch assembly. A company called Quality Trailers makes this particular trailer. They're based out of Ohio. I bought this trailer for roughly $1,250 at a local trailer dealer in New Jersey.

Depending on where in the country you live, you can expect to pay anywhere between $1,100 and $1,400 for a trailer this size. You will see cheaper trailers out there; some of them won't have the pressure-treated deck, and most of them won't have as good of an axle and tires. The trailer we're using is a single axle. You don't need more than one axle to carry what's going to be built on this trailer—the axle is sufficiently robust for you to add a relatively significant amount of weight to the top of the trailer (see step 6).

6. Looking underneath the trailer, you'll see the bottom of the pressure-treated deck and the single axle. The axle is mounted to the trailer by way of a couple of leaf springs. Leaf springs serve as a shock absorption mechanism. If the axle were rigidly mounted to the frame of the trailer, potholes and other road imperfections would transmit rather violently through the frame of the trailer and would rough up whatever resides on the trailer; the leaf springs mitigate this. They also become more effective as weight is added to the trailer (in our case, in the form of a house). When empty, the trailer can feel somewhat bouncy while towing it. That's a byproduct of the leaf springs not bearing a lot of weight.

To build this project, your trailer will need to have a 3,000-pound (1,360kg) rated axle, which means that the axle can safely support up to 3,000 pounds (1,360kg). Understand that the trailer itself has a certain amount of weight. A trailer like this one weighs around 700 pounds (318kg), which means that, before you do anything to it, the axle is already carrying about 700 pounds (318kg). So an axle rated at 3,000 pounds (1,360kg), minus the 700 pounds (318kg) for the trailer, leaves you with 2,300 pounds (1,043kg) of capacity remaining for your build. You never want to max out an axle's capacity. Fortunately, we intend to build something that will bring you to about 2,000

pounds (907kg) of total weight once the structure is complete—well below the max of 3,000 pounds (1,360kg). Note that this 700 pounds (318kg) dry weight presumes that you are not going to keep the fold-down gate at the back of the trailer that generally comes with the trailer.

On less expensive trailers, you may find axles with lower weight-bearing capacities. For example, some trailers come with a 2,000-pound (907kg) axle, and then, if the trailer already weighs 700 pounds (318kg), you can only add another 1,000 pounds (454kg) or so. This puts you in a position where you may not be able to build what you want on top of the trailer. Make sure you know what you want to build and buy a trailer with an axle to support it.

7. This trailer has rather large wheels. They make this trailer highly suitable for what we're doing. These are 15" (38.1cm) rims with a full-size tire. Bigger tires mean more weight capacity and safer towing.

The only time you should ever entertain getting a trailer that will be built near the maximum capacity of the axle, or a trailer with smaller wheels, is if it's going to be sitting in your backyard and you never intend to move it. But if you want to do any traveling with your tiny build, then opt for the robust combination of a strong axle and bigger tires.

The structure that I created on top of this particular trailer wound up weighing right around 2,200 pounds (998kg), or 800 pounds (363kg) below the limit of the axle. I drove that

structure to a variety of places in the United States. All told, I traveled about 6,000 miles (9,656km) with the house and never had a problem. Spending the extra money on a quality trailer pays off. Look around where you live and see what's available. It doesn't have to be from the same company where I purchased my trailer, but look for the characteristics outlined here:

- 5' wide x 10' long (152.4 x 304.8cm)
- Pressure-treated wood deck
- Angle iron rail
- Axle with capacity of 3,000 pounds (1,360kg)
- Large wheels (15" [38.1cm] rims)

STEP-BY-STEP BUILDING THE SHELL

Trailer Leveling

Before you do any building on the trailer, you'll need to level it. As you add building materials to the top of the trailer, use a level to see that you're building everything level and true. The only way to do that effectively is to level the whole thing right from the beginning.

8. At the front of the trailer, you have the hand crank, which raises and lowers the trailer onto the hitch of the tow vehicle. Make sure this end is secure before continuing.

9. Start by placing jack stands under the back two corners of the trailer. Then use the hand crank at the front to tilt the front of the trailer up. By cranking the front end of the trailer up when you have the jack stands under the back corners, it tips the trailer back onto the jack stands, creating pressure, and this in turn takes weight off the tires. This has the added benefit that the trailer will bounce less while you're working on it.

10. In this photo, you can see in the background how a good amount of the weight is off the tires. The trailer should be cranked up on the jacks with the bulk of the weight off the tires the entire time you are working on the project. This doesn't mean that the tires should be in the air and able to spin freely. Having multiple contact points with the ground ultimately aids in stability.

11. Once you have the trailer secure on the jack stands, getting the trailer perfectly level is a matter of trial and error and using a level. The top rail is an excellent spot to place the level. Here you see the level right over the wheel well.

12. Check the level on the sides as well as the front and back of the trailer. You want the entire thing to be nice and level. Once you've leveled out the trailer sufficiently, you can get to the more interesting work.

Initial Trailer Work

In this phase, we'll be assembling the wood siding along the sides and front of the trailer as well as assembling the bump-outs over the wheels.

13. Note the empty areas that are part of the raised rail structure on the trailer. They will need to be filled in, because you can't have a big open space like that in your home.

14. Provisionally clamp a 2x12 piece of lumber vertically to line up with the side rails, one on each side. This will provide an effective barrier between the inside of the trailer and the outside elements. For this part of the 10'-long (304.8cm) trailer, make sure to purchase 12' (365.8cm)–long 2x12s. You can see that this one sticks out the back of the trailer. That's because buying a 10' (304.8cm) piece would actually be just a hair shorter than it needs to be, which wouldn't work. (This is a quirk of standard lumber measurements—see the chart on page 58.) The goal here is to close in the side, so it has to be long enough.

15. Here's a closer look at this clamped 2x12. There is already a pretty decent seal at the tops and bottoms just with the clamping. Don't worry about the vertical uprights in the angle iron rail; those are going to be on the outside, and, since we're running a single continuous piece down the side of the trailer, they aren't in play.

When you already have the top rail (the angle iron) as a flat surface and add a 2x12 in an upright fashion right next to that surface, you're creating a roughly 3" (7.6cm)–wide flat surface that runs the length of the trailer. This will be a great base for mounting the rest of the structure.

16. Sometimes the top of the angle iron rail and the 2x12 don't line up precisely if the top of the rail isn't exactly 12" (30.5cm) up (or rather, 11½" [29.2cm] up), and all trailers are unique. In such a situation, which is what I'm facing here, you will need to make the top of the 2x12 and the top of the angle iron flush. To do this, put some thin slats underneath the 2x12 onto the pressure-treated deck. This will raise the top edge of the 2x12 a little bit, bringing it level with the angle iron rail. These slats are essentially 1½" (3.8cm)–wide strips of wood in whatever thickness is needed to create the level top.

17. Use two of these slats on each side of the trailer, one at the front (hitch) end and one at the back, with a gap in between. This doesn't need to be one long continuous piece, since the main goal is to level the 2x12 with the top rail. The slat is merely a means to that end. Using a piece of wood in this fashion to level something is also called "shimming." The main goal is to even things out before mounting anything permanently. Once everything is mounted, the slats/shims don't play a vital role anymore. Most likely they will continue to be held in place by gravity or pressure, but at that point they will have done their job and fulfilled their purpose.

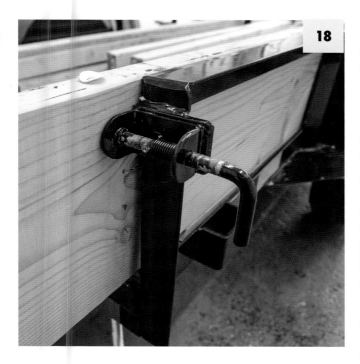

18. Here's another look at this assembly, in which you can see how the 2x12 is flush with the top of the angle iron, the slats sit at the bottom between the 2x12 and the trailer bed, and the 2x12 extends beyond the end of the trailer.

Once you've filled in the first side of the trailer, duplicate the same thing on the other side of the trailer (if you haven't already). Then fill in the front (hitch) end of the trailer as well. Slot in another 2x12 to span the width of the trailer at the hitch end, and slide the side 2x12 pieces back enough to make room to fit the front piece in front of them. Important: Make sure you're following this instruction closely—the rough ends of the sidepieces should butt up against the flat of the front piece. Also leave a little space (about ¾" [1.9cm]) for some plywood to go in between the front 2x12 and the trailer itself (which will occur in step 34). Then cut down all the lengths to match and fit the trailer: cut the front 2x12 to the full trailer width, and cut the side 2x12s ¾" (1.9cm) shy of flush with the back of the trailer (see step 27). This final arrangement of the side and front pieces is partially visible in several of the following photos.

19. Now it's time to start mounting the bump-outs over the wheel wells. These are made with 2x12s that are mounted horizontally outward rather than vertically. Please note that I often use a piece of scrap 2x12 as a placeholder for this process, and that's what I'm doing here when you only see what appears to be a short section of wood in the images.

20. These bump-outs will run the length of the trailer from front to back or, more precisely, from the front edge of the front 2x12 all the way to the back end of the side 2x12s. (Again, I'm using a short scrap piece in this photo, not the full final piece.)

21. As you can see, a good 3" (7.6cm) of this new horizontal 2x12 are lying flat on top of both the angle iron and the tops of the 2x12s that fill in the sides and front of the trailer.

22. Another reason that this kind of trailer works so well for a camper tiny house is that it has outcroppings of angle iron where the taillights are mounted. This is an incredibly robust structure, especially when coupled with the tops of the wheel wells, which are also very solid. The 2x12 bump-outs that are mounted horizontally will rest on this outcropping and the wheel well, making them very stable.

If you have a trailer with a less rigid side structure than this, consider making the bump-outs less prominent. That can be accomplished by using something less wide than a 2x12, such as a 2x10, 2x6, or 2x4. You don't have to include bump-outs at all if you don't want to, but they have advantages: they look good and create more interior space.

23. Here is a full view of the sides filled in, the front filled in, and two test pieces for the bump-outs clamped horizontally at the front.

24. Here is a clear photo of the gap at the front that was intentionally left in step 18, which has been reserved to fit a piece of ¾" (1.9cm)–thick plywood. Remember, nothing has been fastened at this point; this is a dry fit to make sure that you've cut the pieces to the right lengths and that everything lines up.

25. All the full pieces are now in place, including the full-size 2x12 horizontal bump-out pieces instead of the short placeholders.

26. Before you proceed to installing the pieces, paint and seal the sides and edges of the wood that will be exposed to the elements. This applies to the following: the exterior side of the front piece, the exterior sides of the sidepieces, the rough edges of the front piece, the rough edges of the back ends of the sidepieces (visible in the photo for step 27), and the undersides of the bump-out pieces. I opted for a natural, grayish, aged look here (which, in this photo, has only been applied to the front and sides so far, not the bump-outs). This sealing needs to be done before fastening anything to the trailer itself, because you're not going to be able to access all the parts of the wood that will be exposed once you bolt these pieces to the trailer.

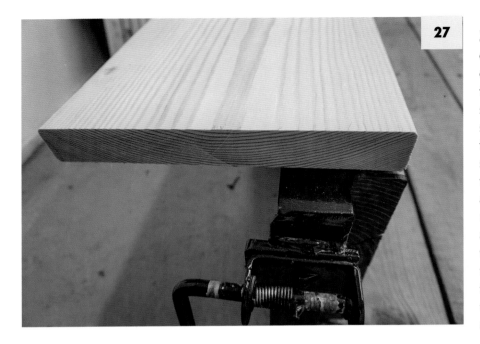

27 **27.** A vertical sidepiece (with sealed edge), the angle iron, and the bump-out piece are all lined up at the back of the trailer. The bump-out and sidepiece should be cut to the same length as shown and not cut flush to the back of the trailer. Leave about ¾" (1.9cm) of space at the back. That's where the back wall of the tiny house is going to be attached; the back wall will be a vertically mounted piece of plywood. If we went all the way to the back of the trailer, we wouldn't have that ledge, and the back wall would be floating in the air. We want the back of the trailer and that plywood wall to be flush with the back of the actual metal framing of the trailer.

28 **28.** Here is one more view of the bump-out piece resting on top of the taillight mount. You'll also have to stain and seal the entire underside of these bump-out pieces, though in this photo I have not done it yet. Remember, you should not have attached anything permanently to the trailer at this point! You need to make sure that everything fits perfectly first. The gaps at the front and back are awaiting their plywood walls, and that's what we'll measure and cut next.

Front and Back Walls

Now we're going to cut and shape the front and back walls of the trailer using pieces of ¾" (1.9cm) plywood.

29. Here is the finished result for the front wall, so you have an idea of what you'll be shooting for. You'll immediately notice that it is in two uneven parts; this is simply because I used 4' x 8' (121.9 x 243.8cm) sheets of plywood. I did it this way in order to get full use of one sheet of plywood instead of wasting wood on two sheets. But you can do a mirror seam down the middle if wasting wood isn't a concern for you.

The front wall, as you can see, is lined up in vertical halves, but the back wall, which you will see later (see step 49), is lined up in horizontal halves. The vertical seam of the front wall allows the front wall pieces to slot in more easily to the front of the trailer. Also, the front of the trailer bears the most force when you're driving, so it is best for both of the pieces to be mounted into and onto the trailer itself, which is only achievable with a vertical seam. In the back of the trailer, the seam will be horizontal, which will help the structure resist shearing. Shearing is a force that the trailer will be subjected to on the highway. There is a lot of wind pressure that forms on flat surfaces heading in the direction of travel. Bracing the structure in various ways helps to dissipate that force and strengthens the structure. The framing helps; the outer plywood skin of the house also helps.

Using plywood as an example, a sheet of plywood is made up of multiple thinner "plies" (hence the name). The strength is not in each thin slice but rather because the grain alternates layer by layer of the plywood (horizontal and vertical). In that same sense, we do what we can to make this structure as strong as possible, and one of those strategies is to mount the front of the trailer with vertical pieces of plywood and the back wall with horizontal pieces. This helps (among other things) to enhance overall rigidity.

To make the front wall, take two 4' x 8' (121.9 x 243.8cm) sheets of plywood and put them down on some sawhorses. Carefully measure the width of the front of the trailer, which determines the width of the very bottom of what you see here (the shortest width of the very bottom of the pieces—the wider sides reflect the bump-outs).

Next, measure the depth of the trailer from the floor to the top of the flat angle iron rail; in this case it is roughly 11½" (29.2cm). That is how far up the shortest width bottom section should go.

Finally, measure the full width of the trailer including the bump-outs to the sides. This is how wide the widest part of the front wall should be.

30. Measure and map the final shape and measurements onto the plywood sheets, and then use your jigsaw to cut out the shapes. Don't worry about the curved top yet, just cut it straight all the way up. Measure twice, cut once—plywood is expensive. Be diligent and methodical. In the end, this is not particularly hard—it's just a matter of doing the calculations and double-checking them.

Plywood Wall Construction

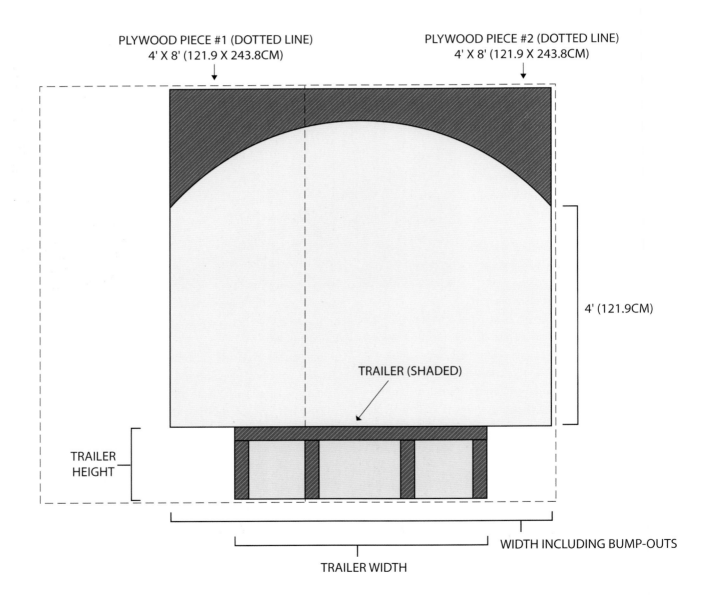

PLYWOOD PIECE #1 (DOTTED LINE)
4' X 8' (121.9 X 243.8CM)

PLYWOOD PIECE #2 (DOTTED LINE)
4' X 8' (121.9 X 243.8CM)

4' (121.9CM)

TRAILER (SHADED)

TRAILER HEIGHT

WIDTH INCLUDING BUMP-OUTS

TRAILER WIDTH

31. Now it's time to create the arc at the top. The arc starts on each side at 4' (121.9cm) up the widest portion of the plywood (not 4' [121.9cm] from the very bottom of the plywood).

32. Draw a line straight across the two pieces of plywood at this 4' (121.9cm) mark. In this photo you can see the line, though I have already cut the arc. Measure this line and make a note of its length. In my case, it is 79" (200.6cm).

So, how can you get that nice-looking, even arc? To execute it, you'll add a nail to the horizontal center of the front wall, attach a string to it, add a pen to the end of the string, and then trace the arc using the nail and string like a protractor. But before you can do that, you need to figure out where to place the nail vertically and how long to make the string. For that, you need a bit of math.

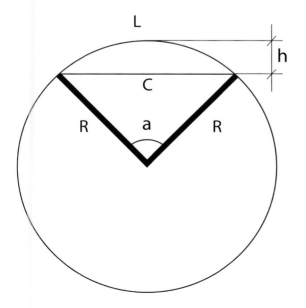

33. The entire half-moon arced area we'll create above the line you drew is what is considered a "circular segment." We already know the "chord" (c) of the circular segment: that is the straight line you measured in step 32, which in my case was 79" (200.6cm). We also know that we want the "arc length" (L) (the curved line) to exactly match the aluminum sheeting we'll be using for the roof. The sheets are 8' or 96" (243.8cm), so that's our arc length. Given these two dimensions, we can use an online calculator to figure out the radius of the circle represented by the arc (R). (My favorite online calculator is *www.planetcalc.com/1421*.) The resulting radius, for me, is about 45¼" (114.9cm).

STEP 33 CONTINUED ON PAGE 74

STEP 33 CONTINUED FROM PAGE 73

Tie the string to that nail and tie a pen to the end of it, making sure the final string is 45¼" (114.9cm) long (or your radius number). Then use a little trial and error to place the nail correctly, ensuring that if you sketch an arc from the 4' (121.9cm) mark on one side that you will perfectly hit the 4' (121.9cm) mark on the other side. In the end, you'll need to place the nail roughly half to two-thirds of the way down from the very top of the plywood.

If I have managed to completely confuse you with this and you are looking for a more rough-and-ready alternative for creating the arc, then let me offer the following suggestion. If you cut a roughly 2" (5cm)–wide strip of thin ¼" (0.6cm) plywood lengthwise (in other words, an 8' (243.8cm) strip), you can use that as a proxy for what will be your 8' (243.8cm) sheet of aluminum roof. We want to stick to 8' (243.8cm) because that's going to be the size of the metal roofing material, and we don't want to cut that roofing material if we can help it. Hold each end of the 8' (243.8cm) strip at the aforementioned 4' (121.9cm) height mark on the wall. Since the distance between your 4' (121.9cm) marks on both the left and right sides of the wall are less than 8' (243.8cm) apart, your strip of plywood will naturally have to form an arc to bridge those two points. That will be your 8' (243.8cm) arc based on your width. Get someone or something to hold it securely in place for you and gently trace that arc outline onto your plywood. Take care to make sure that the arc is straight and smooth and doesn't droop or flatten on one side or the other. This low-tech method, if done well, can yield the same result as the more complex mathematical approach outlined previously.

34. Cut the arc using a jigsaw. Now it's time to dry fit your front wall sections into the trailer! Here is the thinner vertical piece sitting in the gap you left at the front of the trailer.

35. See how it slots in nicely between the 2x12 and the angle iron rail?

36. And see how nice and flush the plywood sits at the front corner in relation to the bump-outs?

37. When you put both front wall pieces in there, you can very clearly see the nicely defined front for this tiny structure.

38. And here's the back view of the front wall. You can see that the plywood covers the ends of the bump-outs on the sides of the trailer. Nothing has been attached at this point, but we're getting closer to affixing all this wood to the trailer permanently.

39. Since the plywood is going on the exterior of that front 2x12, we're going to have to protect it as well. While the plywood is slotted into the trailer, apply some painter's tape on the plywood right along the top edge of the angle iron rail. This way you will know what portion of the exposed plywood needs to be painted and sealed for protection from water damage: everything below the painter's tape.

Plywood does not stand up to weather very well, so seal it as effectively as you can. To that end, paint the inside edges of the seam between the two pieces of plywood as well as all the outer edges and even the bottom edge where the plywood crops out horizontally onto the sides of the trailer. Make sure that you limit the amount of exposed wood in order to avoid wood rot.

40

41

40. The next step for the front wall of the structure is to make some cutouts for the roofing beams. Those cutouts are going to be done in the exact shape of a 2x4, because that's where we're going to use for the roofing beams. Use a scrap piece of 2x4 to measure the slots. The top roofing beam slot, pictured here, falls directly centered on the apex of the arc (see step 33).

41. To mark each slot, simply trace the outside of a scrap piece of 2x4 held in place as shown, flush with the curved edge.

42

42. Once you've determined where the center roofing beam goes, add two more slots to each side of it, plus a third slot on each side that will be married up with the side walls. However, that third slot is not going to be made using a 2x4— instead, it will utilize a 2x6. Let's focus on cutting the five main slots first—the center slot and the two slots on each side of it. Make sure that there's equal spacing between each of the slots, so measure the length of the arc and crunch the numbers to get it right. This photo shows the final cutouts in their correct locations (though the fifth one closest to the camera isn't visible).

43. Now let's talk about the final, third slot on each side of the center slot: the slots that are on the outer side edge of the front wall and that will line up with the side walls when they are installed. As I said before, we're not using a 2x4 for this; we're going to use a 2x6 held flush against the wall edges rather than inserted into the wall like the other slots. This is because the arc of the roof will continue past these side beams. Align and trace a 2x6 so that about one-third of it falls above the horizontal line at the end of the arc (as shown), then cut out the slot.

When we are working on the roofing beams later, we will use a table saw to create an angle on the top edge of these structural 2x6 roofing beams, essentially a portion of each cut out at a 45-degree angle to continue the curvature of the roofline. If we used a 2x4 in this scenario, slicing a third of it off, it would weaken the structure on the side, making it prone to bowing and flexing. For that reason, we use 2x6s instead.

44. Dry fit a 2x4 in each of your five main slots. You want the 2x4 to have a snug fit, snug enough that you need a hammer to make it fit. We'll eventually be reinforcing this—the beams aren't going to just sit in these cavities—but the tighter the better. This is also to minimize gapping that can result in water coming inside.

45. Also make sure that the top of the 2x4 is flush with the arc that you've created—you don't want the 2x4 sticking out of the plywood and creating a bump, because the metal roof is going to go right over this arc. Any bumps or protrusions will cause serious problems.

46. Make the back wall of the trailer in the same overall shape and with the exact same cutouts. As I mentioned in step 29, the back wall should also be cut out of 4' x 8' (121.9 x 243.8cm) plywood sheets, but this time the seam should be horizontal rather than vertical. If you did an excellent job with the front wall, you could simply use your cutouts as a template for the back wall. Be careful, though, because the front and the back of the trailer might not be exactly the same. Definitely measure everything to be sure it will fit properly.

47. In this image the front wall pieces are resting on top of the uncut plywood that will be used for the back wall pieces. Even if you have to fiddle with other measurements for the back wall compared to the front wall, you should be able to simply trace the arc from the front wall—you won't have to mess around with the pencil and string and nail again.

48. Make sure that the measurements and cuts for the bump-out sections are correct, as I'm doing here.

49. Dry fit and clamp the bottom back wall piece in place. It mirrors the same shape and structure as the front wall, with the cutouts for the bump-outs.

50. Here's the other side of the dry fit back piece. We don't have a door cut out yet, but at this point the goal is to line up the back wall with the inner edge of the angle iron on the trailer. Rest it on the back lip of the metal portion of the trailer and make sure that the back wall cutouts for the bump-outs line up perfectly with the horizontally mounted 2x12s on either side of the trailer.

Mounting Everything Thus Far to the Trailer

At this point, we've cut out significant portions of the structure of the trailer, and everything has been dry fit. We're finally ready to mount everything to the trailer permanently.

51. To mount the pieces to the trailer, we're going to use carriage bolts. It's important that you understand what these are and why they're the right choice here. A carriage bolt is a threaded bolt, usually dome-headed on one side, that fastens to something by way of a nut. The threaded section can be in different thicknesses and lengths. To use carriage bolts, you need to first drill through whatever materials you are connecting. For our purposes, we're passing a bolt through 1½" (3.8cm) of wood (the actual thickness of the 2x12s) and also through the angle iron. After that, we still need some of the threading exposed so there is room to thread on the nut. A 2" (5cm) bolt would be too short, because you already have 1½" (3.8cm) for the wood and are adding almost ½" (1.3cm) for the angle iron, leaving

basically nothing left over. The right length to choose here is 2½" (6.4cm). In terms of thickness, go with ⅜" (1cm)–thick carriage bolts.

52. You will also need to allow room for a washer between the nut and the wood, ideally a split washer (which can be seen in the far left of this photo). A split washer has a cut through one side of it so that when you tighten the nut, you're squeezing the two ends of the washer back together again, which creates additional tension and pressure for a better bond. That means a more stable structure and a lesser chance of bolts loosening, especially for a structure that is designed to be mobile.

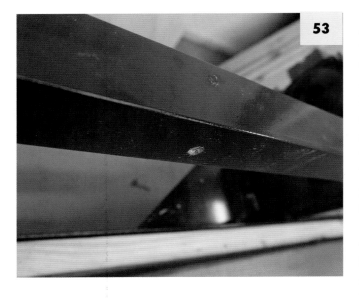

53. It's time to drill the mounting holes. Start with the boards that are vertical in the trailer (the side and front 2x12s). Ensure that the top of each 2x12 is flush with the top of the angle iron (as you did back in step 18), with whatever shimming below the board in place. Then clamp the 2x12s in place with a standard C-clamp or spring clamp. The goal is to keep the boards from moving while you're permanently attaching them. Now drill through the sides from the outside (iron) to the inside (wood). To suit the ⅜" (1cm) carriage bolt, drill ⅜" (1cm) holes. In this photo I have removed the wood piece, but you can see the neat hole I've made in the angle iron.

Make sure that you have the right drill for this kind of work. Not all drills are capable of drilling through the angle iron; it's a tough metal, so if you just have a wood drill bit, for example, you'll destroy your drill bit without making a whole lot of progress on the hole. A cobalt steel drill bit will be up to this task.

54. Once you've made it through the angle iron, you will hit the 2x12 and continue straight through it. Provisionally put one of the bolts through the hole, nut side sticking out the metal exterior. Loosely spin the nut onto the end of the bolt; the purpose here is not to hold it firmly in place, but just to ensure that the hole in the wood and the hole in the angle iron stay lined up as you continue to drill holes.

On the side of a 10' (304.8cm) trailer like this one, drill about four holes total: two or three bolts to either side of the wheel well. Every time you finish a new hole, push a bolt through it to prevent any shifting. This ensures that the holes you drill won't come out of alignment.

55. Once you have drilled and temporarily secured both sides (the front will be dealt with later), move onto the bump-outs. Lay your 2x12 bump-outs, cut to length, on top of the assembled sides and line everything up so that the inner edge of each bump-out 2x12 is flush with the interior flat side of the side 2x12s that you have just temporarily mounted.

Clamp in place and repeat the same drilling process as you did for the sides in order to connect the bump-outs to the angle iron, drilling straight down—that is, drilling down through the bump-outs and the angle iron, not through the bump-outs and into the side 2x12s. Drill down all the way through the 1½" (3.8cm) of the bump-out board thickness, through the angle iron, and out; again, use 2½" (6.4cm) carriage bolts so that you have enough space for adding the washer and nut. Position these holes nicely centered on the angle iron rail, which for me was about 2¼" (5.7cm) in from the inner lip (the flat interior sides of the 2x12s).

If it's not too awkward an angle, drill up from the bottom. This will ensure you don't accidentally end up in a tight spot where you can't get the nut onto the bolt because part of the trailer is in the way (yeah, I've done that). Instead of measuring it out and figuring out exactly where you want to drill through, the easier thing to do is find the easily accessible spots on the underside and then drill up through from there. To make sure nothing shifts as you work, once you have your first hole through the angle iron and the 2x12 bump-out, put a temporary carriage bolt through it. Drill about four holes total along the length of each bump-out, two on either side of the wheel well.

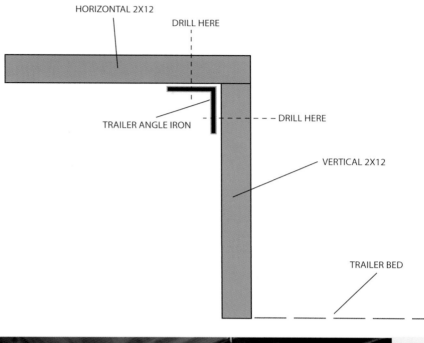

Overlapping Boards Illustration

HORIZONTAL 2X12

DRILL HERE

TRAILER ANGLE IRON

DRILL HERE

VERTICAL 2X12

TRAILER BED

56. Here is a close-up of one area of completed drilled and fastened boards. Try to offset the top-down bolts from the horizontal bolts as shown; in other words, if you put a horizontal bolt 6" (15.2cm) from the back of the trailer, then go 12" (30.5cm) in for the first vertical bolt. Staggering the bolts like this provides more strength and stability to your build. This isn't super critical, but it's a good practice for a mobile structure.

Once you've drilled all your holes, it is finally time to attach the pieces permanently. If you haven't already stained/painted and sealed the wood, do it now, because once the pieces are connected, you won't be able to get in there with a paintbrush to do the work. Remember that any exposed wood will be subject to the brutal vagaries of nature. I like using glossy black paint because it tends to match the trailer's angle iron.

57. In many of these pictures, such as this one, you can see a grayish substance squeezing out between the board and the angle iron. This is another measure against the elements: silicone sealant. You don't want water to infiltrate your structure. Leaving an area unprotected that is prone to water seepage, like right next to this angle iron, is a bad idea. The silicone creates a seal between the wood and metal.

Once you're ready to attach the boards, run a bead of silicone along the edges where wood marries up with angle iron before attaching. I overdid it a little; you don't want it to squeeze out quite as much as I have here in the pictures. Then, once you've mounted that interior board, also run some silicone along the top surface of the angle iron. Do one board at a time: run the silicone along the inside, pop your board into place, put the carriage bolts through (always with the mushroom head/flat side on the side with the wood), pop the split washer on the outside of the bolt, spin a nut on there, tighten it all up, and add silicone along the top. (You want silicone wherever wood and metal come together. Don't worry too much about the bottoms

of the vertical 2x12s where they meet the trailer deck. We'll make sure later that we create a good seal there as well.) I use a socket wrench to tighten up the nut, but a regular wrench or adjustable wrench will accomplish this task just as well. Keep tightening. You may see some of the silicone start to squeeze out from in between the metal and the wood. This is a good sign—it means that you're reducing that space considerably.

58. As you're adding and tightening boards, you may see some gapping at the bottom of the 2x12s where the board doesn't seal quite as well with the metal of the trailer, compared to the nice, tight connection at the tops of the 2x12 where it has been attached to the angle iron. As you continue to tighten the bolts at the top, you will continue to pull the 2x12s tighter to the metal, and any gaps will be reduced or eliminated. If there are any remaining gaps, we will remedy them shortly with some lag screws (see step 66).

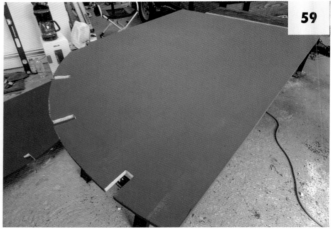

59. Now that we've taken care of the sides and bump-outs, it's time to tackle the front and back sections. The front wall (hitch side) needs to be painted and sealed before being attached, as it will be exposed to wind and water; not only should you have a good exterior seal, but also a seal on the edges as well. Here you can see that I've painted and sealed most of the edges and the large surface area; I still have to seal the slots for the roofing beams, so don't forget to do those, too! At the top of this photo, you can also see the black section that I painted back in step 39, which will be exposed through the front framing of the trailer.

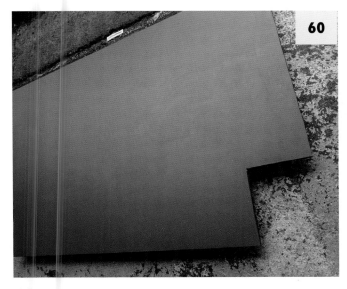

60. Here is the lower section of the back wall, painted and sealed.

61. And here is the upper section of the back wall. Again, I haven't sealed the slots yet, but you need to do so!

62. Slide the front wall pieces into place between the front 2x12 and the trailer, and follow the same drilling, bolting, and silicone sealing process as described previously for the side boards and bump-outs. Drill horizontally through the 2x12 and the angle iron, this time using 3¼" (8.3cm) carriage bolts, to account for the extra ¾" (1.9cm) thickness of the plywood front wall. Use about four bolts across the entire front piece.

63. As with the side 2x12s, you may need a slat/shim between the bottom of the front 2x12 and the trailer deck (visible at the bottom left). As I described earlier, the point of the slat/shim is to line things up. I generally don't make an effort to remove them or to permanently affix them. Most of the time, they continue to stay exactly where they are even when they've completed their task of making things align.

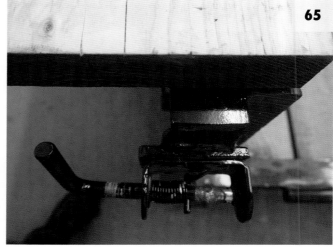

64. At this point, you have permanently installed the side and front 2x12s, the bump-outs, and the two plywood pieces comprising the front wall. It's starting to look like something!

65. You may remember that we left a little bit of space at the back end of the trailer in step 18, shown here, to accommodate the plywood back wall that we're going to be putting there. It's important to check that the ends of the side 2x12s and the bump-outs line up flush with one other. Double-check this now.

66. These are lag screws, which are intended to go straight into the wood and don't need a nut (hence the pointy bit on the one end). We will use these and some 2x4s to tighten up the sides in the following steps. You will need lag screws that are 2¼" (5.7cm) long.

67. This particular trailer has several hollow metal outcroppings on its sides. These are used for tie-downs for things that you are transporting on the trailer. They happen to be the exact size to fit a 2x4.

68. Cut small sections of 2x4s (in this case, 13" [33cm] long), drill a hole in roughly the middle of each one (all the way through) for a lag screw, and slide each one in from underneath (up through the hollow metal outcropping), all the way up to the angle iron as shown in the next photo.

69. You can see here how the 2x4s fit beautifully into the outcroppings. Screw the lag screws in through the 2x4s and into the 2x12s. To do this, first drill clear through the 2x4 while holding it in place (you already drilled through in the previous step), and stop right after you hit the underlying vertical 2x12. That leaves a mark from the drill on the 2x12 where the continuation of the 2x4 hole is. Use a smaller drill to drill about a ½" (1.3cm) hole into the 2x12. That small hole allows the lag screw to pass through the 2x4 and then grab the surface of the 2x12. As you tighten the lag bolt, this screwing will tighten up the gaps at the bottoms of the side 2x12s by pulling the 2x12s up snugly against the 2x4s.

70. Now it's time to attach the back wall. If you haven't painted/sealed the upper and lower back wall sections yet, do so now. You can see here the lower back wall section mounted up against the 2x12s. The cutout perfectly adheres to the contours created by those 2x12s, pressing against both the edges of the bump-outs and the edges of the side boards.

71. Use some temporary screws there to attach this lower back wall section to the 2x12s on both sides as shown, using about five screws per side. These screws are just a temporary way to attach this piece of plywood to the back of the structure while creating the door and other features. We will be creating a more solid, permanent connection later, since we'll be linking the side-wall framing elements with the back wall and tying it all together. Right now, we just want the back wall to stay in place.

71

You've now temporarily attached the lower back wall section, but before you can add the upper back wall section, you have to make a decision about the width and height of the door. The height of the door is determined by the overall length of the 2x4s you use to frame the sides of the door. Since those 2x4 framing elements of the door run from the bottom (floor) to the top of the doorframe, they are what becomes the initial mounting point and connector between the bottom piece of plywood in the back wall and the top piece that sits above the bottom piece (see step 72).

I'm 6' 3" (190.5cm) tall, and I don't mind ducking through a door. Unless you are a giant, I suggest your door height be between 5' (152.4cm) and 6' (182.9cm). To match the proportions of this structure, I made my door 5' 8" (172.7cm). As for the width, assuming you have a 5' (152.4cm)–wide trailer, go with a door of 24" (61cm) to 26" (66cm) in width. You don't want to create a door of a standard width and height because it won't be proportionally correct for a small structure like this.

72

72. I chose 26" (66cm) as the width for this door. Place vertical 2x4s, cut to your desired door height (5' 8" [172.7cm] in my case), at 26" (66cm) apart from each other to frame the door. This serves to attach the upper back wall section to the lower back wall section. Glue the 2x4s to the lower section of plywood and attach them with some temporary screws through the outer side. Do the same with the upper section of plywood, carefully making sure the pieces are flush. This forms the full back wall.

Now your build has a front wall and a back wall. The back wall does not yet have a door cut out, which comes next. In the meantime, you'll have to get in and out of your build by climbing over the bump-outs.

Doorway

To finalize the door cutout area, you have to connect the two vertical 2x4s with a header 2x4 piece that bridges them at the top. That top portion will complete the outline of the final doorway.

73. I have already cut out the doorway in this photo (and added roofing beams; ignore them for now!), but you can see how there is a horizontal 2x4 resting on top of the two vertical 2x4s. Cut and place this 2x4 and temporarily screw it into place.

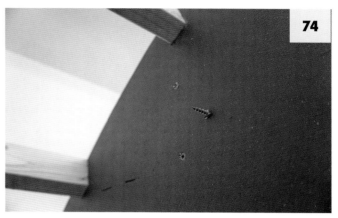

74. Now run a screw in each the four corners of the rectangle formed by your framing 2x4s, from the inside to the outside, so that they poke out the front as shown here. This will show you the dimensions of the doorway on the painted exterior of the structure, which is helpful so that you can draw straight lines between these points and then cut that door shape out by following the lines. Seeing this on the exterior side will also allow you to visualize where the 2x4s of the doorframe run behind that plywood. Now is a good time to run about 15 or so 2" (5cm) screws through the exterior plywood and into the 2x4s that comprise the doorframe. That ensures that plywood wall and the doorframe are permanently connected with one another.

75. The bottom two screws should be right up against the trailer bed as shown here.

76. Since the back wall plywood has already been mounted to the trailer, you have to do the cutting vertically rather than with the plywood horizontal on a set of saw horses. You can use a jigsaw to cut out the doorway, but I recommend using a router and a bit with a ball bearing on the end. To use this method, first drill a hole into the cutout area. Put the router bit through that, and then simply follow along the 2x4 edges with the router to make a nice, neat cutout. Your doorway is done!

Roofing Beams

With the back and front walls in place, it's time to cut and place the roofing beams into their slots!

77. Assuming you have a 10' (304.8cm) trailer, take five 12' (365.8cm) 2x4s and cut them down to 11' (335.3cm) in length. Place them into the slots with the front ends flush with the front wall and the extra 1' (30.5cm) of beam sticking out on the back of the house. This will create an overhang, which is nice to have because it acts a bit like a mini porch overhang when it's raining. (In this photo you can also see the two 2x6s on the very ends, which we'll deal with shortly.)

Overlapping Roof Material

THREE 4' x 8' (121.9 x 243.8CM) ALUMINUM SHEETS

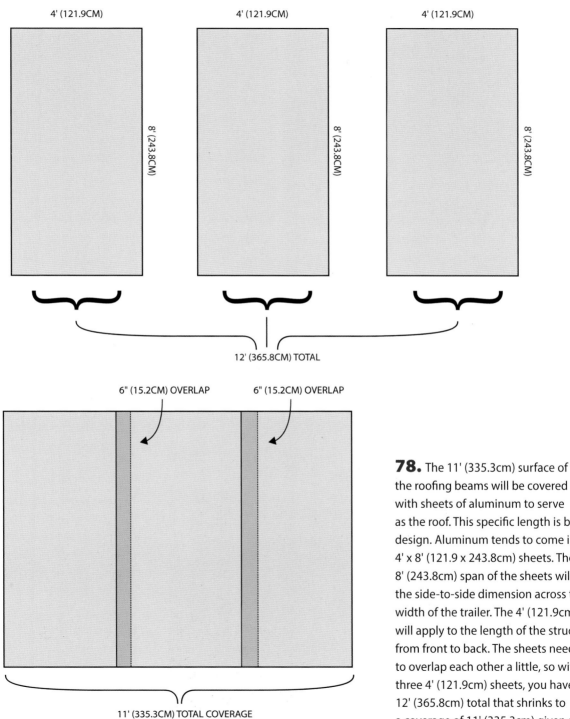

4' (121.9CM)   4' (121.9CM)   4' (121.9CM)

8' (243.8CM)

12' (365.8CM) TOTAL

6" (15.2CM) OVERLAP   6" (15.2CM) OVERLAP

11' (335.3CM) TOTAL COVERAGE

78. The 11' (335.3cm) surface of the roofing beams will be covered with sheets of aluminum to serve as the roof. This specific length is by design. Aluminum tends to come in 4' x 8' (121.9 x 243.8cm) sheets. The 8' (243.8cm) span of the sheets will be the side-to-side dimension across the width of the trailer. The 4' (121.9cm) span will apply to the length of the structure from front to back. The sheets need to overlap each other a little, so with three 4' (121.9cm) sheets, you have 12' (365.8cm) total that shrinks to a coverage of 11' (335.3cm) given a 6" (15.2cm) overlap between each sheet.

79. Now for the two side beams, which are composed of 2x6s instead of 2x4s. Cut these beams to 11' (335.3cm) long as well. These 2x6s are also going to need a 45-degree angle cut from the top portion to follow the arc of the roof. For this kind of work, I prefer to use a table saw. If you don't have access to a table saw, you can use a rotary saw; most of them will allow you to change the angle of the blade by changing the footing piece. There's really no other good way to cut this piece, and this is one of the very few cuts in the build where it's hard to beat the convenience of a table saw. You can see in this photo how the blade is angled to 45 degrees.

80. With this 45-degree cut completed on the entire length of each 2x6, the 2x6s will now slot perfectly into their cutouts. These 2x6s retain a lot of rigidity and strength even though they have been partially reduced.

81. With the 2x6s in place, you have all seven roofing beams completed. Since the 2x6s don't have a slot that will reliably hold them in place on the sides, run a screw through the front and back of each 2x6 directly into the plywood of the wall. That will hold them where they need to be and ensure that you don't get whacked in the head by one if it decides to fall from its cutout perch.

Squaring Up Front and Back Walls

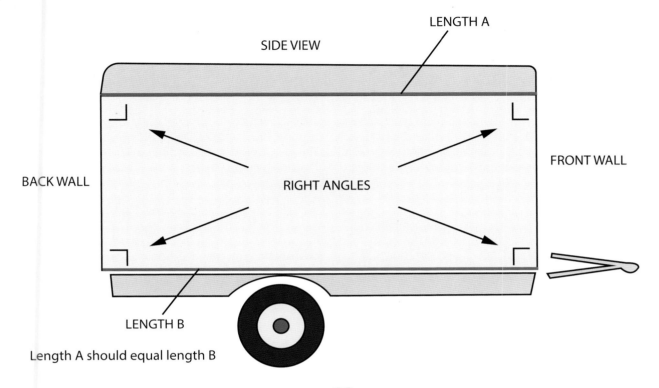

SIDE VIEW

LENGTH A

FRONT WALL

BACK WALL

RIGHT ANGLES

LENGTH B

Length A should equal length B

82. Now it's time to level the top and bottom. Start by taking two measurements: the distance from the front wall to the back wall along the topmost roofing beam, and the distance from the front wall to the back wall along the bed of the trailer. These should be close to 10' (304.8cm), but get an exact and accurate measurement for each. In the end, these measurements need to be the same. Similar to how we leveled the trailer initially, we now need to make sure the essential skeleton of the structure is straight and true. We want the front and back walls to be standing straight up and forming right angles both at the peak and at the floor. It's important to be diligent while placing the roof beams, because you don't want to have the front and back walls squeeze together at the top and be further apart at the bottom where they meet the trailer. Adjust the beams as needed to ensure that the measurements match and that everything is square before continuing.

Side Walls

Now that the roofing structure is in place and the doorway has been cut, it's time to frame up the side walls. The exterior walls will be supported by a framework of vertical 2x3s, the studs, that are mounted between the 2x6 roofing beam and the outer edge of the bump-outs, with an added 2x3 between the bump-out and the bottom of each vertical 2x3. You can see this 2x3 mounted vertically on its side in step 83. Since 2x3s generally come in 8' (243.8cm) lengths, use a full length and another piece about 23" (58.4cm) long to span the length of a 10' (304.8cm) trailer. To mount this "bottom of the wall" 2x3, apply construction adhesive between it and the 2x12 bump-out

and then run 3" (7.6cm) screws up through the 2x12 into the 2x3.

See page 95 for a preview of what the completed wall will look like so that you have the visual in mind as you proceed. The side walls are there to lend rigidity to the whole structure, but given that these walls are only 4' (121.9cm) in height, 2x3s, rather than 2x4s, are the best choice for the studs; you save both money and weight. We're also not going to use the 16-on-center building standard construction where structural 2x4s are spaced 16" (40.6cm) apart when measured from the middle of one 2x4 to the next. Instead, we're going to be spacing the 2x3s in a closer configuration.

83. Start by marking the exact middle of the 2x12 bump-out: measure from the front wall to the back wall, divide in half, and mark the middle. Cut the 2x3s you need as described in the previous paragraphs to the correct length to fit snugly in one continuous length along the bump-out from the front to back wall. Mark the middle of this continuous 2x3 length as well, and place it on the bump-out. Here you can see the 2x3 sitting in position, perpendicular to the 2x12 and running along its outer edge.

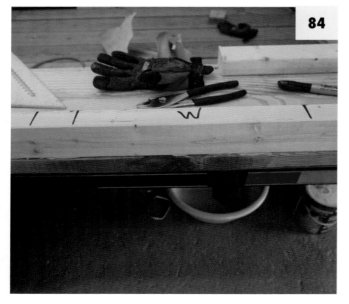

84. Working off the middle, decide how far apart to space the 2x3 studs. For these side walls, I went with 12¼" (31.1cm) between each 2x3, because there's a particular window that I like to include in this build that is 12" (30.5cm) square, so I need there to be at least 12" (30.5cm) between each stud. If you're following my measurements, then measure roughly 6" (15.2cm) out from the marked middle in both directions. Mark those lines. Those are the edges of the first two 2x3 studs. You've just created the space for your first/centered 12" x 12" (30.5 x 30.5cm) window. Since a 2x3 is 2½" (6.4cm) in actual width, mark this accordingly. You've now marked out your centermost space, with a window, and the first studs to each side of it. The big W marked in this photo is my indicator that a window will be going above in this space.

85. From the edges of the 2x3 markings, mark out another 12¼" (31.1cm) in each direction. There, mark your next 2x3. Continue like this until you've done the entire length of the trailer. You will have about eight freestanding 2x3 studs plus an additional two studs that will be flush with the front and back walls. The final freestanding stud is not going to be a perfect 12¼" (31.1cm) from the previous one; it will be closer to the front or back wall, but that's fine, because you're not placing a window into that last framing pocket anyway. (You've marked eight studs now, but see step 90—you'll be adding the two additional flush studs to each side at the end.) Based on how many spaces between studs you've now created, you can determine where and how many windows you can and want to place. If you're working off of an 8' (243.8cm) trailer, you will only be able to put in two windows of the size we're using here. But on a 10' (304.8cm) trailer, the spacing will allow for three windows. I recommend maximizing the number of windows, even if they are just small windows.

86. Now repeat this entire measuring and marking process on the 2x6 roofing beam that's directly above the 2x3 we've placed along the bump-out. This will help ensure that the 2x3 studs will be perfectly vertical as you match them to the top and bottom markings. Finally, repeat the entire measuring and marking process on the other side of the trailer at both top and bottom.

Next, measure to check the overall total height of the walls. This should be measured from the bottom of the angle cut on the 2x6 roofing beam, down to just past the bottom edge of the bump-out 2x12 at the bottom. This height should be 4' (121.9cm) or very close to it. The structure has been designed this way because we want to be able to cover the sides of the structure with a standard 4' x 8' (121.9 x 243.8cm) sheet of plywood. We don't want an unnecessary seam, which would happen if we exceeded the 4' (121.9cm) side wall height.

If a 4' (121.9cm) side wall makes you think that the interior is going to be a place where you bump your head a lot,

it's not. Keep in mind that this 4' (121.9cm) wall is actually about 1' (30.5cm) off the floor of the structure. So roughly 5' (152.4cm) is the lowest point on the very sides of the interior. Since there is an arched roof, the center height is upwards of 6' (182.9cm). I'm a tall guy, so I pretty much refuse to build anything so small that I can't personally be comfortable in it— and I'm comfortable in this build!

87. It's simple to figure out how long to cut your 2x3 studs. The total wall height, as described above, should be 4' (121.9cm). Delete from that the following measurements: the 1½" (3.8cm) thickness of the 2x12 bump-out at the bottom; the 2½" (6.4cm) thickness of the marked-up 2x3 sitting on top of the bump-out; and about 4" (10.2cm) of the 2x6 roofing beam below the angle cut. This all adds up to 8" (20.3cm). Subtract this 8" (20.3cm) from the total wall height of 4' (121.9cm), and you are left with 3' 4" (101.6cm). This is the length of your 2x3 studs.

Whatever the exact measurement winds up being for you, measure and cut your collection of 2x3s. Cut them a bit long at first so that you can adjust the length to perfection. This is like LEGOs™, except you're the one creating the pieces. Cut four more than you think you'll need, because we're going to add four more in step 90.

Toe Screwing

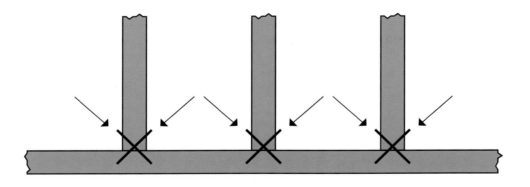

Screw through the bottoms of the upright studs
to attach them to the bottom beam

88. It's time to permanently attach the 2x3 studs to the marked-up 2x3 beam and the 2x6 roofing beam. Since you can't go all the way from the very bottom up through the 2x12 bump-out and the 2x3 beam and get into the vertical 2x3 stud, you're instead going to send the screw diagonally through the sides of each 2x3 stud. This is toe screwing. Place the 2x3 studs in the locations that you've marked and then toe screw them into place to the 2x3 beam with 3" (7.6cm) screws, two per stud coming from opposite sides of the stud. These screws are long enough to pass through part of each 2x3 stud diagonally and still anchor properly into the 2x3 beam. Repeat the toe screwing to secure the tops of the 2x3 studs to the 2x6 roofing beam.

89. In this photo you can see one of the screws going in diagonally.

90. Add one additional 2x3 stud directly butted up against and attached to the back and front walls on each side. This adds additional strength, plus it is also your opportunity to create a stronger connection between the side wall, front wall, back wall, and the side roofing beam. Seal between the stud and the plywood with silicone sealant.

91. Here is a fully assembled side.

92

92. At this point, we have the front and back wall, we've framed out the side walls, and we have all the roofing members in place. We're in good shape, and it's starting to look like an actual house!

Roof Dry Fit

The next step is dry fitting the aluminum roof. The roof will comprise 4' x 8' (121.9 x 243.8cm) aluminum sheets in either 20-gauge aluminum or 18-gauge aluminum. (This may be sold or referred to as 0.032 and 0.040 thickness, respectively.) I prefer to work with the 20-gauge since it's the best trade-off between thickness, easiness to work with, and price. The 18-gauge is a bit thicker. When you buy your aluminum roof, take a look at both to see if you have a preference.

Aluminum is light and easy to work with. I buy my sheets of aluminum through a local branch of Metal Supermarkets. Depending on the thickness you choose, you can expect to pay somewhere in the realm of $100 per sheet; we need three sheets for this 10' (304.8cm) build. Aluminum sheeting is fairly

readily available compared to some other roofing materials, like copper.

You could use a piece of thin Luan ¼" (0.6cm) plywood for the roof instead. (Luan is a generic name for a particular type of thin plywood.) This is certainly even easier to get at your big box hardware store, but it will be harder to seal properly and won't last as long. The gypsy wagons that inspired this particular build style traditionally had cloth roofs, and you could do that as well, although it won't lead to a relevant weight savings, given how the rest of the structure is constructed. There are ways that you can treat and apply epoxies to cloth to form a rigid covering for the roof. I've never used either of these alternative roofing methods, so I can't recommend them, but if they suit your particular purposes, feel free to give them a try.

93. This roof, as we've discussed before, will consist of three overlapping sheets of aluminum that completely cover the roof and roofing beams, including overhangs (see the illustration on page 89). At this point we're just going to do a dry fit to make sure everything is shaping up correctly. You have seen me apply this strategy a number of times during the build: lay everything out to see if it all fits where it's supposed to before attaching anything permanently. Here is the back wall, with the 1' (30.5cm) overhang.

94. Here you can see where two of the aluminum sheets overlap one another. Remember that the overlap should be 6" (15.2cm) between sheets one and two and 6" (15.2cm) between sheets two and three, which will result in a total roofing coverage of 11' (335.3cm), the entire length of the roofing beams.

95. It's likely that when you first lay the sheets onto the roof, they're not going to fall neatly into place. It will take some flexing and prodding, but the material is soft and pliable, allowing for easy and forgiving manipulation. Just be careful not to bend or crease the material, since you won't be able to easily repair imperfections you might create by doing so.

96. I typically use a small scaffolding (visible to the right) to put the roof on, since I work on my own most of the time. The roof placement is one of the harder parts to accomplish alone, so I highly recommend that for this part of the build, you enlist somebody for the day or for a few hours to help you. Maneuvering these large sheets of aluminum is tricky. They're not particularly heavy, but their size makes them cumbersome. You certainly don't want to drop them, because that will dent or bend them (which is hard to fix).

97. Here's an inside view of what it looks like when two of the sheets have been laid in place.

98. Here is the inside view again with two sheets in place, facing the front wall.

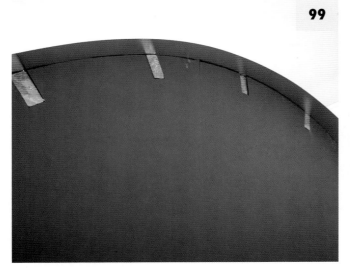

99. At the front of the trailer, your 2x4 roofing beams are flush with the plywood wall. On this end, include about 1" (2.5cm) of aluminum overhang. You don't want any more than that because it will capture too much air while you're driving on the highway; anywhere from ½" (1.3cm) to ¾" (1.9cm) to 1" (2.5cm) will do. This overhang is necessary to cover up those roofing beams on the front. You have a lot of exposed area there, and water can infiltrate the seams where the metal touches the plywood and where the 2x4s sit in the cutouts. When the time comes, you will need to seal this up well.

100. I like to place a decorative piece of cedar trim on the ends of the exposed 2x4s on this front wall. If you want to do the same, cut out a 2" (5cm)– to 2½" (6.4cm)–wide piece of cedar that's about 4" (10.2cm) to 4½" (11.4cm) long and place it on top of each of the 2x4s in their slots. Although this is a good stage at which to cut these pieces out, I don't suggest mounting them just yet. The ideal stage when you should attach them (using construction adhesive, silicone, and a finishing nailer) is when you have fully attached the aluminum roofing. That's when you'll be in a position to fully seal the front of the structure (i.e., where the metal roofing touches the front wall plywood).

101. As we are in the thick of finishing the roofing, now is also a good point at which to finalize the fastening of the roofing beams to the plywood. As you recall, the five cutouts for the roofing 2x4s were done in such a way that each 2x4 is seated snugly in a cutout. Since you have full access to these before doing the roof and ceiling, now is a good time to add a bit more adhesion and strength to this portion of the build. Use steel rafter ties for this; they are pieces of steel with a 90-degree twist. You mount the top part to the side of the 2x4 and the other part to the plywood wall. Use 1½" (3.8cm) screws for mounting into the 2x4 and ¾" (1.9cm) screws for mounting into the plywood walls, since longer ones would pass clear through the walls. Add one of these rafter ties, front and back, to each 2x4 and 2x6 that comprises the roofing structure. This is yet another way to solidify and add strength to the build and the walls, which was something I referenced we would be doing back in step 71.

102. Here you can see the front wall at a later stage, with all the trim pieces in place, along with the front window. The front window is actually what we'll be doing next.

STEP-BY-STEP BUILDING THE SHELL

Front Window

You can use any number of different kinds of windows for the front of your structure. I put a rather large window there. At first you might think this is counter-intuitive because it is in the direction of travel as you tow the house. But this window is exactly opposite the door and serves as a secondary means of exit from the structure in case of an emergency. If there is a fire or an obstruction that keeps you from getting out the door, you can leave through this window—the 12" x 12" (30.5 x 30.5cm) windows on the sides are too small to fit through, nor are they openable by design, whereas this large front window can be opened and closed, allowing for air circulation. I chose a used RV window, readily available on eBay. The shipping cost

is relatively high for these because they're heavy, bulky, and cumbersome. This window happens to be a two-section slider window. You can slide the one side open, and there's a screen in it. I highly recommend you get a window with a screen, because when you're going for ventilation, you don't want bugs to get into your place. This particular window has a lip, which is essential to the window installation instructions that follow. There is an inner frame that corresponds to the size of the actual window hole, and there is a ½" (1.3cm) to ¾" (1.9cm) flat lip around the exterior of the window. You will send a few screws through that exterior lip to attach it to the wall.

103. Outline the cutout of the window on the front wall. This is as simple as running a pencil line around the inside edge of the wide, flat lip of the window. This will allow you to attach the window along its wide outer lip and form the area that creates the seal for the window opening. The black metal framing portion of the window itself is typically made of powder-coated aluminum, as is the case with the window I'm using here.

104. Cut out the window hole using a jigsaw. The jigsaw is the tool of choice here because the interior side does not have framing yet and because these windows usually have rounded corners, which would need to have rounded framing behind them for the router to follow the window cutout outline.

105. After you have made the cutout, frame it with 2x3s. This way, when you drill and screw through the sides of the RV window and into the plywood front wall, the screws will have something to bite into that's more solid than just the plywood.

106. Directly below the window is a 2x4 that connects from the floor of the structure (or rather, the 2x12 vertical front piece) up to the framing of the window. There is another 2x4 above the framing of the window, which terminates at the top edge of the plywood front wall. These 2x4s cover the seam in the front wall, which increases the wall's strength and rigidity. Measure and cut your 2x4s to length after installing the window. If you're working alone, glue the 2x4s in place, allow them to dry, and then put a screw through from the outside in. Having a helping hand on the other side would make it easier—instead of waiting for the glue to dry, you could have someone hold it in place while you screw.

107. Here is the installed window from the outside.

108

108. This image also provides a good view of another feature I've added at this stage. I've effectively created a right angle with two 2x3s here in the corner section, where the side wall meets the back of the house, by adding a new 2x3 right in the corner in all four corners of the house. You can install these new 2x3s now. Screw the bottom horizontally into the 2x3 that sits perpendicular to the 2x12 bump-out; screw the top horizontally into the 2x6 roofing beam. Further lock these 2x3s in place by sending some 1¾" (4.4cm) screws through the plywood side, since that will lock the front and back wall to the side wall framing and complete the connection we first referenced in step 71.

These added 2x3s are not structurally necessary, but they will make attaching the interior walls easier to do at a later point. Having a clearly defined corner on the interior creates a termination point for the interior wall to attach to. Without it, the end of the interior wall (front or side) would dangle in the air. Having the additional perpendicularly mounted 2x3 in each corner eliminates this and creates a contiguous mounting point that carries around the entire interior of the structure. The walls will all be 1½" (3.8cm) thick, and doing this in the corners ensures that the 1½" (3.8cm) thickness measurement is true for all parts of the wall, while also providing the aforementioned interior wall termination and end mounting point.

Electrical

Although my goal throughout this book has been to keep the initial shell build section separate from the section that will cover what you turn the shell into, there is one aspect that straddles both: electrical. While you don't need to have a completely finished structure in mind when you install the electrical system, it does need to be considered at this point. This is because it is the one thing that you can't really do after you insulate and close up the interior walls. Electrical wiring runs inside the walls and therefore needs to be put in place at this juncture. If you already have a good idea of where and what kind of electrical your structure will need, that's great. For the purpose of keeping it simple, I will outline an electrical layout with the items you will need and an overview of what the electrical setup will comprise. This will remain rather basic, since basic will be the most conducive system regardless of what you decide to turn your tiny structure into.

A word of warning: if you are in any way uncomfortable working with electrical components, then bring in an electrician to assist you with this portion of the build. If you want to stick to a limited budget, the best advice is to do the bulk of the electrical install yourself and then hire an electrician to look over your work before you ever run any electricity through the system. That way, you don't have to pay the electrician's hourly rate for things you can physically do yourself while still having the peace of mind that comes with having someone with greater knowledge look the system over and potentially make any changes or modifications in the places where you may have done something not quite right.

The electrical setup that I'll be showing you incorporates both AC and DC elements. This basic setup could also be amended to include solar power. I have installed this basic system in numerous tiny builds, and it has always worked well for me. We'll start with the general layout of the electrical setup and then go into more detail on the various components and installation instructions.

109. If you are completely uncomfortable with the whole subject of installing an electrical system and really don't require much access to electrical in the house, then simply run a cord through the wall into the house. That will give you access to a single place to plug in devices (assuming that the house is connected to a power source, an extension cord, externally).

110. The electric connects to the exterior of the house through a docking point like this one (which is more resistant to water and rodents than simple a hole for a cord to pass through). All you are doing with this most basic solution is making an external electric source available inside the house. This requires absolutely no knowledge of anything electrical. But if you're interested in some kind of installed system, keep reading.

111. Take a look at this overall basic electrical scheme. The terms "on grid" and "off grid" get thrown around a lot in the tiny house scene, and the setup shown here incorporates elements of both. The on-grid component will supply you with power to 110-volt (110V) electrical outlets when you are connected to an exterior electricity source. This means when the house is plugged in or connected to a generator. There is also an off-grid component in the form of a battery, since it is nice to have some flexibility to use power even when you are not connected to an external power source. This battery will allow you to use 12-volt (12V) power to light the house via the ceiling lights as well as to run some limited-power devices such as USB charging ports and potentially a small fridge or fan. Before installing the door or window or closing up the walls, install whatever electrical you plan to include in the structure. This means both the 110V AC wiring as well as the 12V DC wiring and all associated features such as outlets.

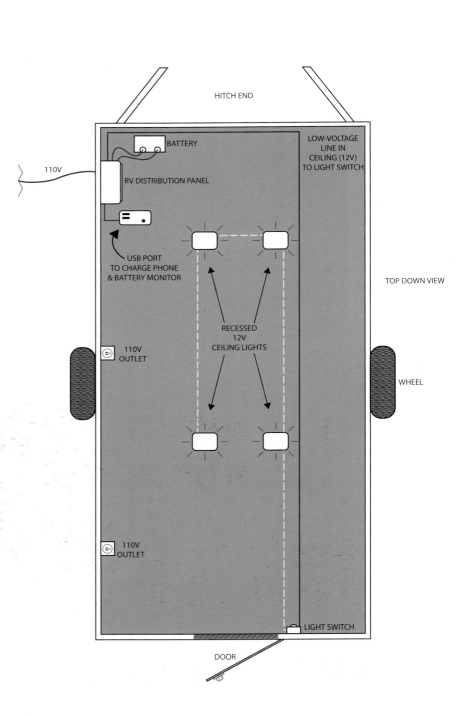

112. To run the 110V AC wiring to the electrical outlets, drill through the 2x3 wall studs. If you don't do that, you will be exposing the wiring, which is not very pretty, nor is it good practice to have live (albeit insulated) power running exposed throughout the structure.

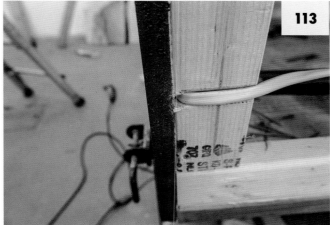

113. In places where the electrical line has to make a turn, chisel out a piece of the 2x3 stud so that the wire can sit in that nook, wrapping around to the outside and back through the stud toward the interior (toward the doorway, in this particular case). If you don't create this nook for the wire, you will not be able to apply the piece of plywood (the exterior side wall) flush to the outside of the stud, because the wire will get in the way.

114. Install electrical outlets onto the sides of the studs. Make sure they are positioned far forward enough that they will be accessible when you have finished adding the interior wall paneling.

115. The 12V DC wiring is used for the recessed ceiling lighting. Run this wiring up the front wall and into the ceiling.

STEP-BY-STEP BUILDING THE SHELL

116. The electrical control panel will eventually be installed between the bed and the seating area (see page 150), but it's worth explaining now. All of the wires in the house should converge in this electrical panel, including the 110V AC wiring and the 12V DC wiring. This panel connects to the external power source, to the battery (see the next step), and to a USB charging station (see the next step). There are a number of different panels available for this purpose. In the one I use, I run the external power into a set of breakers. Those breakers are what the 110V AC lines to the interior outlets emanate from. The breakers are also there to power the 12V DC side of the panel that handles all of the low-voltage needs.

116

117

117. The battery is your backup power. This battery will eventually be installed in the front right corner, under the bed (see page 150), but again it's worth explaining now. When the camper is plugged into an external power source, that source will supply electricity to the battery, charging it. When you're not connected to an external power source, the battery will provide some electricity to the house, mainly just for the 12V functions. The 12V system is what runs the ceiling lights as well as a USB charger. On the USB charging port there is also a battery monitor. The battery monitor is simply a gauge that indicates how much power you have in reserve in your battery. They come in different formats. A basic one represents charge in the form of percentages (i.e., 75 percent charged). Others will give a voltage that the system currently has so that you can see if voltage is on the high or low side (i.e., 13.5V = high; 12V = low).

Closing up the Side Walls and Adding Side Windows

Now we're ready to start working on the side walls; it's all coming together. The side walls will be made of standard 4' x 8' (121.9 x 243.8cm) sheets of plywood; you will need three sheets. You don't need as thick plywood for the side walls as you do for the front and back walls; those walls were made with ¾" (1.9cm) plywood, but for the side walls, use ½" (1.3cm) plywood. Plywood comes in all different types of grades. Choose the smoothest surface texture that you can find, and avoid pieces that have big holes and knots in the top layers, since they just won't look as nice. Don't confuse particleboard and chipboard for plywood. Those are the sheets that look like a jumble of bits and pieces of wood all pressed and glued together. That's exactly what they are, and they are not suitable for this build.

118. I chose to paint the side walls the same color as the front and back of the house. As with the front of the house, we will cut the windows after the walls have been fully mounted, not before. For this build, a 4' x 8' (121.9 x 243.8cm) sheet will not be enough to cover the 4' x 10' (121.9 x 304.8cm) side of the house. Each side will be composed of one full sheet plus a 4' x 2' (121.9 x 61cm) piece of another sheet. So, you'll need a total of three sheets: two full sheets and one sheet to cut into pieces for either side.

119. Use glue and screws to attach the plywood sheets to the sides of the build. You should screw in four places: at the top on the 2x6 roofing beam, twice on the 2x3 studs, and at the bottom into the 2x3 directly below and perpendicular to the 2x3 studs (on top of the 2x12 bump-out). See step 130 for a visual of this. Use 1½" (3.8cm) to 1¾" (4.4cm) screws so that they won't protrude on the interior, but will instead end within the 1½" (3.8cm) thick wall framing of the 2x3 studs. In this image, you can see the 2' (61cm) gap in the side wall where the first 8' (243.8cm) sheet of plywood has ended.

120. Include a liberal amount of construction adhesive on the outside surfaces of the 2x3s and the 2x6 roofing beam to ensure an even stronger bond between the exterior plywood and the framing members. This is always good practice when building tiny buildings, given the rigors they will be subjected to on the highway. Safety is paramount. I always tend to "overbuild" for this reason, since the alternative is not a good one.

The full 4' x 8' (121.9 x 243.8cm) plywood sheet should end in the middle of a 2x3 stud; if yours doesn't, cut your sheets to sizes that will ensure this. Not only should you apply construction adhesive to the surface of the 2x3 here, but also apply clear vinyl caulking right at the edge of the sheet of plywood. When you put the additional 2' (61cm) piece in place, squeeze it up tight against the first plywood sheet and make sure it is flush all the way from top to bottom. This will ensure that water infiltration is kept to a minimum at this seam.

121. Now it's time to put some windows into the side walls! Fit a piece of 2x3 into one of the gaps that's designated for a window, right up against the 2x6 roofing beam, to create the top framing for the window. The vertical 2x3 studs have already created the side framing for the window. Remember, these windows are 12" x 12" (30.5 x 30.5cm). When you are done cutting out the window opening, you will put another 2x3 at the bottom of the window to complete the framing (this is in step 125).

122. Test the fit by inserting the window into the interior space under the top framing 2x3 to make sure there are no issues before proceeding to affix it permanently. While it's up, mark the bottom line for the cutout.

123. Similar to what you did to cut out the door, drill screws into each corner to create the frame for cutting out the window from the outside. You'll note that the screws on the right-hand side are a little bit on the inside of that 2x3 stud; that's because I was a little bit generous in the sizing of the spacing between the 2x3s. It's perfectly fine.

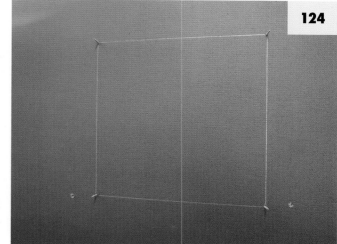

124. Here's the exterior view of the screws marking out the window space. The four screws come all the way out through the sheathing of the structure. Mark around these screws to draw the window cutout. The other screws visible in this photo are the ones that have attached the plywood sheathing to the studs.

If your vertical 2x3 studs on the interior formed a perfectly snug frame around your window, you could at this point add a 2x3 framing piece along the bottom of the window just like you did at the top and then use a router to cut out the window opening, like we did for the doorway. However, since the framing was a bit too generous (there was too much space between the 2x3 studs to create a perfect fit for the window opening), we have to go the more manual route here. If we followed the easy router method, we'd cut a hole that was too wide. Remove the screws and use a jigsaw instead to create the window cutout.

125. Repeat this entire process for each of the three windows on each side of the house. In this photo, you can see that there is side framing and top framing to the windows; I have yet to do any bottom framing on these. Go ahead and do that now.

126. It's time to install the six windows into your completed frames. I actually ended up waiting until after I had installed the roof (which is the next step), so you'll see the windows missing from the cutouts for the photos in that section, but now is a good time to put them in. The windows I used have pre-drilled holes for screwing them into place. Make sure you are happy with the fit before proceeding with the permanent install. Before installing, seal the windows for moisture and insulation. Run clear silicone sealant on the back of the window itself, right where the lip extends from the actual window piece. Then pop the window into place. The silicone will squish out between the frame and the plywood that you're mounting it onto, forming both a bond and seal. Then screw the window in using 1½" (3.8cm) to 1¾" (4.4cm) screws. If you use anything longer, you run the risk of them passing all the way through the 2x3 framing.

127. After the window is screwed in, I like using a thin cedar trim to go around the outer edges. Again, I did this after putting in the roof, so you won't see it in the photos for the next section, but you could basically install this whenever you want, and we'll install more of it at the very end of the build. You could use any decorative wood or a synthetic material, like a PVC product. These trim pieces are optional, but they aren't just decorative: they also add another layer of defense against water infiltration.

128. I create these trim pieces using a table saw. I purchase the cedar planks in 8' (243.8cm) lengths that are ¾" (1.9cm) thick and 5½" (14cm) wide. They are intended to be used as porch/decking material. Cut the planks widthwise into 1½" (3.8cm)–wide strips, and then cut them again to reduce the thickness—cut the ¾" (1.9cm) dimension in half to achieve a thickness of about ⁵⁄₁₆" (0.8cm). Keep in mind that the thickness of the saw blade further thins these strips. This is known as "kerf" (the width of material that is removed by a cutting process). Throw that lingo around to impress your friends. This process is a bit labor intensive, and the table saw really helps to make it possible. It's a great way to turn a single starting cedar plank into a pretty vast amount of trim material, though. You can attach these various pieces with a combination of silicone in areas where you want additional seal and construction adhesive in areas where sealing is less important. Most of the trim serves a functional aspect, though, so there is more silicone used than adhesive. Mount the trim strips with the finishing nailer. That, coupled with adhesive or silicone, holds them in place effectively. For full shots of the final arrangement, see the gallery (page 8).

Attaching the Roof

We've already done a dry fit of the roof, but now it's time to actually install it. It will be installed with the three sheets overlapping, as we've discussed before, with the first sheet laid on the back (door) end, the middle sheet laid next, and the final sheet laid on the front (hitch) end last. Why do we do it this way? For the same reason that roofing shingles are applied from the bottom up: it ensures that when water runs down or across the structure, it runs off it rather than being caught in it. In this case, since this structure is designed to be towed, there is always going to be more water coming from the front (hitch) end and heading toward the back. When you overlay the sheeting in this fashion, the water will travel over the top of sheet number one at the front to get to sheet number two and then three and then off the back of the structure. This will reduce the chances of moisture getting through your roof on rainy-day drives.

129. Referring back to the section on dry fitting the roof (pages 96–99) as needed, assemble the aluminum sheets on the roof. Ensure that the sheets are all squared and lined up, that the overlap is uniform, and that there is a bit of overhang on the hitch end. Once you are sure that the roof material fits and looks right, take the sheets down again and apply a construction adhesive on top of all the roofing beams. This way, the metal sheets will not only be *screwed* into place, but also *glued* into place.

After you place the first sheet on the hitch end of the structure onto the adhesive, run a very thick bead of silicone onto the overlap section (where it will overlap with the second sheet); this will both waterproof the seam and adhere the first and second sheets together. Once the second sheet is on, put another bead of silicone onto its overlap section to similarly bind and waterproof the second sheet to the third sheet.

130. Now it's time for the screws; use 2½" (6.4cm) self-sealing screws, which are a specialty screw that has a rubber gasket that gets compressed when screwed in, forming a watertight seal. You want those roofing sheets to be as secure as possible, so use about five screws per roofing beam per sheet to attach them firmly. In this case, that works out to about 75 screws (three sheets times five beams times five screws). All those little dots you see along the roof in this photo are screws. Don't attach into the two side 2x6s yet. We'll do that bit differently in the following step.

In order to figure out the exact placement for the rows of screws, run a chalk line across the roof along each beam. Nail the little end piece of the chalk line (it's helpful if you have somebody who can assist you with this) to the very front edge of a 2x4 roofing beam at the hitch-end overhang. Walk the chalk line to the doorway end, get on a ladder, find the matching end of the 2x4 beam, and snap a line onto the aluminum. This will create a straight line indicating where to drill the screws into the roofing beams beneath.

131. Where the sheets hit the 2x6 roofing beam on the side, run a thick bead of silicone sealant, since here we are dealing with the end of the sheet and another potential entry point for water. Also, don't use self-sealing screws for this. Instead, use screws that attach the metal to the 2x6 in a flush fashion. You want this to be flush since you are now going to add a cedar trim rail to the roof edge to channel water off the roof. The cedar trim rail further serves to sandwich the end of the aluminum sheeting between itself and the 2x6 roofing beam. The aluminum should terminate around the midpoint of the cedar trim. The trim used here is roughly 1½" (3.8cm) wide and

¾" (1.9cm) thick; it's the same trim used in step 128. Screw through the cedar trim all the way into the 2x6 beam. For this, you will need screws that are about 2" (5cm) in length. You may have to pre-drill those locations since your screws (unless they are self-drilling) will not pass though the metal into the 2x6 roofing beam. As with everything else here on the exterior, run sealant between the cedar roof rail and the metal below so that water can't pass underneath, but instead runs the length of the roof line and is ejected off the front and back ends of the roof. This prevents the water from passing underneath the cedar rail and streaming down the side walls of the tiny house. You don't want that much water hitting those plywood walls and risking wood rot.

Trailer Floor

Let's take a step back and see where we are: we've attached our roof, we've got a front window in, and we've got six side windows in. Except for the door, we've essentially closed out the exterior. Let's now focus on getting the interior prepped.

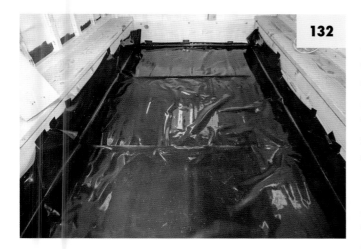

132. The pressure-treated deck in the trailer is a nice base to work from. It requires a vapor barrier, though, because water will be splashing up underneath the trailer. You don't want that water inside the structure—and that's what the vapor barrier is for. Use thick plastic film to create a vapor barrier. You'll find this in the flooring section of most big box home improvement stores. It's effectively the same material as a thick and durable garbage bag.

Roll it out on the inside of the home, making sure it comes up on the sides—up the 2x12 sides and front we installed along the trailer frame way back in the beginning. Tape the film in place along all sides to create a kind of plastic tub. By extending the barrier up on the walls like this, it will be more effective at keeping water out of the home. Since the black plastic material and the tape to affix it are less than attractive running around the lower vertical perimeter of the interior, I always choose to cover this up with appropriately sized sections of thin ¼" (0.6cm) plywood. It covers the plastic liner and tape and creates a visually clean surface. You can either install this plywood now or do so later when the interior is being finished.

133. The layout of the plastic tub-like barrier around the interior is fine for the front and sides. When you get to the door opening, though, you have to cut notches into the plastic so that the lip that extends up the walls all around the structure doesn't create a lip at the door. After you notch the plastic at the doorframe, it will lay flat inside the door opening. Tape it down to the metal back rail that the door opening sits on. The bottom of your door will provide the water seal to keep water from entering under the door. This point will have the least exposure to moisture anyway since you have the roof overhang above and it's located at the back of the trailer and not in the direction of travel.

134. Before putting down the actual final flooring, put down a product that's like a thin foam pad between the vapor barrier and the final flooring to come. (This is a photo of another build I did that shows both the foam underlayment and the flooring being installed on top of it. I neglected to take a photo for this book's build because the floor tends to go in pretty quickly.) This foam underlayment adds some insulation (wall insulation will come later in the Interior Finishing section). For regular homes, the product is usually marketed as being used for sound insulation. This foam also adds a little bit of squishiness and allows the floor to lay nicely flat. After all, the pressure-treated deck that we're building on is not always going to be perfectly flat—it's not designed to be a floor for people to walk on, it's designed for a lawnmower to sit on. This extra layer of foam on top of the vapor barrier and underneath the final flooring helps to even it all out.

135. This is the finished result in the current build. I recommend using flooring that is relatively thin and light. I use engineered wood, which consists of a thin piece of wood veneer on top of some thin plywood. It is quite straightforward to put in; it typically has pieces that click together. Each piece has a grooved pattern on the edges. You lay one piece down, and the next piece clicks into that piece you just put down. You lay the entire floor down in much the same way that you would put together a puzzle. Measure the length of flooring you need to get to the end of the line, and use the miter saw to make the cut accordingly. The piece you cut off becomes the first piece in the next row of flooring you lay down. Keep doing that until you have filled the space.

This kind of flooring is usually sold in boxes designed to cover a certain square footage of area. Work out what your square footage will be. For this build, we have an area measuring 5' x 10' (152.4 x 304.8cm), so we have about 50 square feet (4.6 square meters) to cover. This particular flooring came in boxes that provided 35 square feet (3.3 square meters) of coverage, so I needed two boxes to do the job. Tip: One smart way to get your hands on a small quantity of flooring like this is to check Craigslist or other online marketplaces; people are always selling remnants when they finish up major flooring installs. It's pretty common to have 100 or 200 square feet (9.3 or 18.6 square meters) left over on a large project, which is more than you'll need.

136. Here's a little bit of a side note, an optional change that I made around this stage that I'll explain here. The taillights, which were mounted directly behind the wheel on an outcropping of angle iron (shown in this photo), wound up being recessed too far back for my taste; I didn't like the way that the bump-out of the trailer limited the exposure and visibility of the lights when compared to the previously wide-open see-through way that the utility trailer foundation of our tiny structure was designed to function.

137. So I decided to move the lights further toward the rear of the trailer to make them more visible to vehicles traveling behind the trailer. And I had the perfect mounting point: the additional upright 2x4s that I had slotted into the hollow hitch tubes built into the trailer (see step 69). I simply took an extra piece of wire, spliced it in from where the original mounting point was (shown in the previous photo), moved the taillights to where I wanted them, and reconnected the wires.

138. Here's the taillight on the other side of the trailer. As you can see behind the light, I had to add a bit of extra wood to the original 2x4 to get a nice, solid structure. Don't be afraid to improvise like this when it comes to your own build. Always modify what you are not comfortable with. This is especially true when it comes to matters of safety, as was the case for me with these taillights.

Door

So, we've completely closed in the front and sides with the addition of the windows, and now a door needs to be installed. How complicated or simple you want to make your door is up to you and your resources. You could easily produce a simple Z barn door out of some pine. You could get a solid wood door and cut it down to size for your doorway; I did that in my original tiny house, and it turned out really nice. The door I went for with this particular build is a bit more complicated than other methods, so don't feel you have to follow my lead; you can go with one of the easier options if you prefer! But if you're interested, follow along to see how I achieved a Dutch (or split) door with interesting hardware.

139

139. First let's talk about the shape and style of this door, before moving on to its composition. This is a Dutch door, which means that the top and bottom sections of the door open separately. You can open the top portion while leaving the bottom portion closed. I included a ledge on mine, which is a great place to put a cup of coffee when you're looking out over your wonderful view from the doorway. Constructing a door of this style is actually pretty intuitive. Start by building the door in one piece, sized to fill the entire doorway. When you're doing your measurements, though, factor in the ¾" (1.9cm) thickness of the ledge that you will install in the middle of the door— make your final door piece ¾" (1.9cm) shorter than you actually need to fill the doorway to accommodate the ledge. And, of course, cut the door into the two sections sized as you want. This is not an exact science. Doors can be frustrating, so take your time. A door that sticks or closes strangely will be a constant annoyance. If something isn't working the way you want it to, figure out what's sticking or out of place and try to remedy it. Trimming a bit off here and realigning something over there goes a long way toward getting a sturdy and functional door in the end.

You can see in this photo that I have used two hinges per section of the door; you don't need three, but you do want the hinges to be fairly beefy. The type of hinge that you use will be up to you. These hinges happen to be exterior mounted hinges, and they are of course screwed directly through the back wall's painted plywood and into the 2x4 that frames the doorway. The door can be a real centerpiece for your build, so make aesthetic choices that please you.

140. The ledge is made out of a ¾" (1.9cm) scrap piece of the same material that the front of the door is made of (see step 143). That little groove you see on the bottom front of the door edge is the same groove that overlaps the boards on the front of the door (but it's not important—it serves no purpose, it's just the scrap I had). The ledge is installed by adding some adhesive and screwing straight down through the wood and into the plywood of the core of the door.

141. Speaking of the plywood core of the door, let's discuss the composition of the door itself. The main core of my door is a piece of ½" (1.3cm) to ¾" (1.9cm)– thick plywood. I happened to have some door hardware that I wanted to use, so in order to incorporate it, I made a cutout for the hardware in the sheet of plywood. Because the hardware was thicker than my plywood, and because I didn't want the exterior of the door to simply look like plywood, I covered the entire front of the door with an additional layer of wood, as well as adding a small rectangle of plywood to the back of the door near the hardware only in order to get the full width I needed. Again, this is likely more complicated than what you might want to do, but that's how I chose to do this particular door.

142. Here you can see the size of the plywood rectangle I screwed to the back of the door to accommodate the thickness of the hardware. This is custom work, and if you are building a custom door yourself, you will invariably be faced with scenarios like this where you have to make some on-the-fly tweaks for the hardware you want to use. I won't go into detail about the installation of the actual hardware itself, as that will depend on your particular hardware; just screw holes and make cutouts as needed. You can always find an easier way to do things. For instance, the interior lock could just as well be a latch you slide into place when inside the structure. The exterior lock could just be a padlock. These solutions aren't quite as aesthetically pleasing, but just know that there is always a solution if you are struggling with this kind of aspect during your build.

143. The wood I used to cover the front of the door is ½" (1.3cm)–thick tongue-and-groove untreated pine that came in 5½" (14cm)–wide planks. But I didn't just use it as purchased; instead, I used *shou sugi ban* on the surface to give it a different finish before installing it on the plywood. *Shou sugi ban* is a Japanese wood treatment process whereby you scorch the wood with a blowtorch and then take a wire brush to the burnt sections. (I find it to be a fascinating technique that might be worthy of having a whole book dedicated to it. You can check out some videos on YouTube that provide an overview of the process, if you're interested.) This gives you a beautiful and smooth brown surface. After the burning and scoring, add some linseed oil (after the door has been fully put together), which is a natural product that further seals the wood. Through the burn technique and the linseed oil, you can create a weather-robust surface, with the added bonus that insects will stay away from it: since they're instinctively and naturally predisposed to stay away from fire, the burnt surface deters them.

144. The pine facing is attached to the plywood with a layer of glue and a series of screws. The *shou sugi ban* process takes place prior to this assembly. Apply glue to the front surface of the plywood door and place the pine onto it. It's helpful to use some clamps to hold the pine in place on the front of the plywood. Screw through the back of the door and into the pine, ideally before the glue has dried. (If you send the screws in from the pine side, it would be visible from the outside.) You can see the screws on the inside of the top door section in this photo. Make sure your screws are the perfect length to go all the way through the plywood and part of the way into the pine.

You will also notice in this photo a little scrap lip on the back of the door. That is a placeholder for a lower-profile, more elegant strip of wood that I eventually installed to serve as a stop to keep the top portion of the door from overextending back past the bottom portion of the door. Having it there allows for the top to be open when the bottom is closed and for the whole door to be opened as a single unit, but it prevents the bottom of the door being open while the top is closed, since that configuration isn't useful.

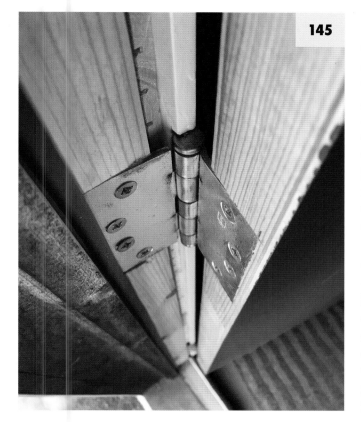

145. Hanging the door is in some ways simple and in some ways complicated. There are many how-to articles and books out there that can teach you how to hang a door in detail and with great precision. It mostly boils down to lots of measuring and dry fitting before you actually drill any screw holes. This is another one of those steps where having an extra set of hands is very beneficial. For a split Dutch door like this one, I incorporate two hinges for the top portion of the door and two for the bottom portion of the door. I mark the locations where I wish to attach them to the door (appropriately spaced). I then transpose these measurements to the doorframe to see the placement there and mark it with a pencil.

You have some options regarding hinges. Most doors typically use a hidden hinge that can't be seen when the door is closed (as shown in this photo). You can also use a surface-mounted hinge, which is the kind that is fully or somewhat visible on the exterior of the house and therefore can often be found in ornate styles. That's what I used here for this build. Using this kind of exterior hinge is definitely easier and more forgiving, since the alignment of the door is easier to achieve and there is no notching or finagling needed to get the hidden hinges to nestle in between door and frame.

Interior Finishing

Now that the basic frame of the house is nearly complete, we can get to work on insulating your home and installing the interior ceiling and wall finishings. On your interior walls, you have several cavities and recessed areas between different pieces of wood. We'll fill those with pieces of compressed foam board to act as insulation, and then cover that with the actual walls and ceiling.

For the insulation, use compressed extruded foam board, which you can buy at any big box store, in a thickness of either 1" (2.5cm) or 1½" (3.8cm). Foam like this has a pretty decent R-value relative to its price and ease of use. R-value is a representation of how much of a thermal barrier the insulation material provides. Insulation efficiency is just a measure of how well a material traps air and how (in)efficient it is in transferring heat or cold. Different insulating materials have different R-values, the higher the better. R-values depend in part on thickness/quantity: a thin layer of a super-efficient insulation may have the same end R-value result as a thick layer of a less-efficient insulation.

146

147

148

146. Cut each piece of foam board to fit each cavity in your walls, as you can see here to one side of the doorway. The pieces of foam board don't have to fit exactly, but do cover most of the area that you see. Try to pressure fit them into place: cut them to the exact size of the opening and then nudge them in, so you don't need any glue to hold them in place.

147. Here is the other side of the doorway, with a cutout around the light switch, of course.

148. Make sure you have all the electrical cords in order before adding insulation in front of them.

149

149. Fill in all the various pockets and cavities in the walls with the insulation material, cutting small pieces to slot in where needed, as shown on the front wall along the top. You don't need 100 percent flawless coverage, but get at least 95 percent coverage.

150. With all the wiring and insulation done, you can close up the interior walls with your final wall product. For my build, I used a tongue-and-groove pine product that comes in 8' (243.8cm)–long, roughly 3½" (8.9cm)–wide, ¼" (0.6cm)–thick pieces. The pieces fit together seamlessly thanks to the tongue-and-groove design. There is a small protrusion on one side of the wood and a slot on the other edge of the piece. The protrusion goes into the slot of the subsequent piece. It's similar to the way that the pieces of engineered flooring slot together to form one contiguous surface. Start from the bottom of the wall and work your way up. When you get to the windows, do the cutouts you need to go around them and fill in all the gaps. Mount all of this to your vertical wall framing using an air tool brad nailer. I use the very thin 1" (2.5cm) brads, since they leave hardly any marking on the pine boards yet form a solid attachment to the framing elements below.

151. Before installing the ceiling finishing, make sure all of your electric up there is wired. I ran wires through the cavities up there for some recessed 12-volt lighting. Also insulate the ceiling before putting in your ceiling finishing. For that I recommend rock wool (brand name Roxul). Rock wool comes in mats of different thicknesses and has the consistency of a loaf of bread. It's water and fire resistant, but it is also an irritant, so protect your skin and respiratory system while working with it. Cut pieces and place them between the 2x4 roofing beams to form a nice, well-insulated ceiling. Make sure that you cut the pieces to a slightly greater size than you need to fill in the spaces—you want a bit of compression, but not too much, on either side of the material to hold it in place. The reason not to compress it too much is because insulation properties don't get better the more of it you cram into an open space. Part of how the material works is based on how it traps air and creates a barrier. It's designed to do that and perform in a state similar to the way it comes out of its packaging. Compressing

it may actually make its insulation properties worse since the compression will modify the material's ability to do its job of trapping air. So if you squeeze it down too much, you will not only use more insulation material (meaning you will spend more money), but you may also be lowering its effectiveness.

152. The ceiling finishing is made of ¼" (0.6cm)–thick pieces of Luan plywood, which also comes in the standard 4' x 8' (121.9 x 243.8cm) sheets, like other plywood sheets. Leave the pieces at their 4' (121.9cm) width, but cut down the length by a few inches, based on the needs of your final structure. This is a trial-and-error process. Cut a few inches off the 8' (243.8cm) side and push the piece into place up against the underside of the roofing beams. The plywood will flex and bend to conform to the arc of the roof/ceiling. If the sheet is too big to cleanly complete that interior arc, trim another inch off and try again to get it into place. Once you figure out the exact size needed for that first sheet, you can cut the remaining two sheets to match. You'll need three sheets total for a 10' (304.8cm) tiny house. Two sheets of 4' (121.9cm) wide will get you to the 8' (243.8cm) mark, and you'll need to measure and cut down the final sheet to cover the remaining uncovered portion of ceiling.

If you are installing recessed lighting in the ceiling, as I have, cut out the mounting points for the lights you are using before attaching the plywood to the ceiling. Cut the holes for your lights in such a fashion that you will be able to access any wiring you have run along the roofing beams to attach your lights to. (This is shown in step 3 on page 134 in the chapter Step-by-Step Building a Camper Tiny House from the Shell.)

You can simply use finishing nails to hold the ceiling panels in place; they usually don't need much coaxing to stay, since the flex in the plywood creates tension. It is, however, a little tricky to get the seams to line up, and you can see in the photo that there is a bit of a gapping between the three pieces on my ceiling. You can clean that up by covering the seams with another piece of trim. You can see this in the second half of the building instruction, on page 134.

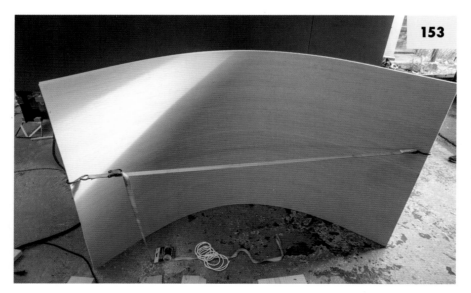

153. If you're having trouble getting the plywood to flex and adapt to the curvature of your roof, put the plywood under tension overnight. In this photo, you can see a couple of pieces of the plywood bent with the help of a tie-down belt hooked into the 4' (121.9cm) sides, creating a bend along the 8' (243.8cm) axis. Leave the plywood like this overnight, and, by morning, there will be a curve in the wood for an easier application to the roof.

154. The basic interior is pretty much finished! This is a good point to say, "Here is your shell." At this stage, you have effectively created a blank canvas for whatever comes next. Congratulations are already in order: you've put together your first tiny house, and it's solid and well built, it looks good, and it's safe. Pat yourself on the back. You are ready to turn this into whatever you dream of it becoming.

Now You Have a Shell— Do Your Own Thing

Congratulations, now you have a shell of a tiny house, and with that shell, you can do whatever you want—the sky's the limit. Now that you've made it this far, it is time to turn that blank canvas into something that suits your wants and needs. Of course, it's also possible that you haven't built the structure yet. You're reading this book to get some ideas and get a feel for what's involved with a build like this. Now is the time to talk about the various things you can turn this structure into.

This book is mainly about building your first tiny house. In the remaining pages, we will ultimately be turning the shell into a structure that you can spend time in, sleep in, and cook in. But don't let my example define your build. On the contrary, I would much rather see you build something that looks entirely different from what I did, and then send me pictures of it. That's what this is really about; it's about creating your unique structure, your unique expression of what it is that you want and need. That's much more important than trying to copy anything that I did here. This is true for all the sections that have preceded this chapter, and it certainly is true for everything going forward in this book.

So, beyond building a livable space, what are some options for you? Let me spark your curiosity and creativity by giving you a few examples of real applications for a structure like this.

Teen space: You can park one of these tiny houses in the backyard and use it as a place for your young or adolescent kids to spend time in (check with your specific local laws and regulations about doing

so). It could be something as simple as a place for them to play video games, or a cozy space where they can hang out with friends. As parents, we're always looking to allow our kids to become more independent. Why not have a space like this in the backyard for your teenager? Sometimes the parent/child relationship can be improved by creating a little bit of space between you and your teen. Ultimately, we want to raise independent kids, and giving them their own space, that they are responsible for, is one way for them to learn the life skills that they'll need down the road.

Home office: You can also turn this build into a backyard office. More and more people have the luxury these days of being able to work from home. Having a dedicated office in your backyard is a great alternative to trying to create one inside your actual house. Maybe you don't have room for one in your house; or maybe you do, but you wind up working at the kitchen table anyway, or you sit on the living room couch and the dog comes over and wants your attention, or the cat crawls all over your laptop. It can be difficult for many people to focus if they're not in a dedicated workspace. Studies show that most people are more efficient and productive when they work within a space that is reserved for work. Therefore, why not create an extra structure to serve as a backyard office? You could even turn it into a place where you see clients, if that is the kind of work you do. Maybe you're a therapist; perhaps you're a vocal coach; or you could do tutoring or homework help there. All these things can be done in a small structure like this, and it can be customized to suit your exact work needs. See a sample floor plan on page 129.

Pool house: If you're lucky enough to have a pool in your backyard, you know what it's like when people are trickling in and out of your house, dripping water all over the floor, waiting in line for the bathroom so that they can change, and so on. Why not pop one of these builds next to your pool and use it as a dedicated pool house? You can have all your clean towels stored in there, a hamper for dirty clothes and towels, a drying rack or mini clothing line for wet bathing suits, and so forth. At the back you can create a changing room, and you could even pop up an outdoor shower on the side of this thing so that people can rinse off. A dedicated pool house keeps traffic out of your actual house and makes it that much easier for you to keep things clean and neat. Plus, it looks nice—it's a beautiful structure to have sitting next to your pool. See a sample floor plan on page 130.

Music studio: I've seen people turn this build into a recording studio. If this is your dream, you'll need to insulate the interior a little bit differently, with acoustic foam on the walls. This build is big enough to fit a drum set, guitar, and some amps, and you can rock out in the structure without disturbing anybody in the vicinity, including your neighbors. See a sample floor plan on page 127.

This space is even tinier than the build in this book, but it serves as a perfect hangout space for up to four people. Imagine what you can do with your build!

Guest space: A guest space is a beautiful thing to have. Maybe your house isn't quite big enough for one, or that room is currently serving as a playroom for the kids and you don't want to kick them out. You could place one of these in your backyard, potentially in the same camper configuration you'll learn later or potentially without as many bells and whistles (or different bells and whistles). Folks staying with you aren't going to have a huge need to cook in there; the predominant function is for them to have a place to sleep and be comfortable in private. Ideally, they will still have access to a shower and bathroom facilities within the house. See a sample floor plan on page 128.

Aging in place: We have an aging population in the United States and other places around the world. There are few solutions for where older people can spend time and be cared for, and many times they are cost-prohibitive. Providing space for aging in place is an excellent way to keep an eye on your aging parents. Giving them a backyard home in a tiny house can keep them safe while still providing a way for them to have their autonomy, their own space, and their independence. If someone is going to be spending a significant amount of time in a structure like this, you will need to contact your local government to make sure auxiliary dwelling units are permitted. See a sample floor plan on page 128.

Workout space: We're all trying to stay healthy. I've seen what happens when you put an exercise bike or a rowing machine in your bedroom or living room: it becomes a rack for your clothing, your clothes hangers, your towels, and anything else you don't know what to do with. And for the most part, that's because it's in a room that you don't think of as an exercise space. You can turn one of these tiny dwellings into a dedicated exercise space and solve the same problem that you solved for a home office:

having a dedicated space for something makes it easier to focus on that thing while you're doing it. When you're in your exercise space, you're not faced with distractions; you don't eyeball the TV remote just a couple feet away or stop in the middle of a workout to feed a begging cat. You can design your exercise space to suit your preferred machines and movements. It could be a straightforward yoga space, for which you don't need to do much more than what we've already built, or construct something more complicated, or put several workout machines in there. You can store whatever implements you use (blocks, mat, weights, etc.) within the structure, too, which will prevent them from getting in your way in your actual house. See a sample floor plan on page 131.

Camper: This is what I'll teach you to create in the remainder of this book. Flip to page 132 to get started!

Floor Plans

Here are a handful of floor plans to show you visually the kinds of things that we have been discussing. Hopefully, you'll find something you like or that can inspire you to draw your own personalized floor plan. Don't be afraid to sketch, sketch, sketch, and don't forget to measure. Have at it!

The scale for each of these floor plans is 1":15" (2.54cm:38.1cm).

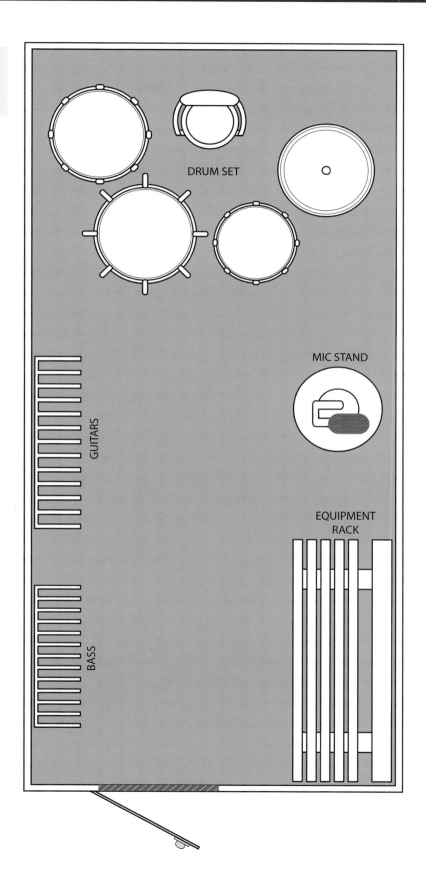

DRUM SET

MIC STAND

GUITARS

EQUIPMENT
RACK

BASS

NOW YOU HAVE A SHELL—DO YOUR OWN THING

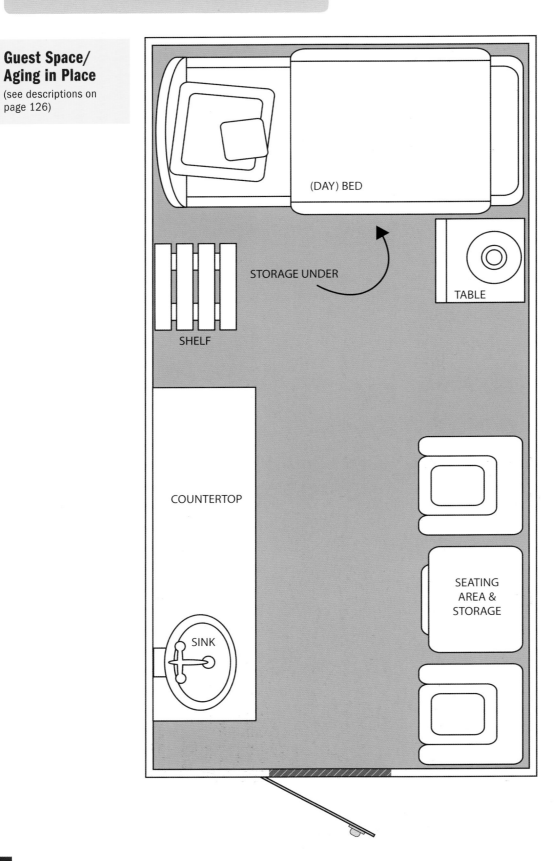

**Guest Space/
Aging in Place**
(see descriptions on
page 126)

(DAY) BED

STORAGE UNDER

TABLE

SHELF

COUNTERTOP

SEATING
AREA &
STORAGE

SINK

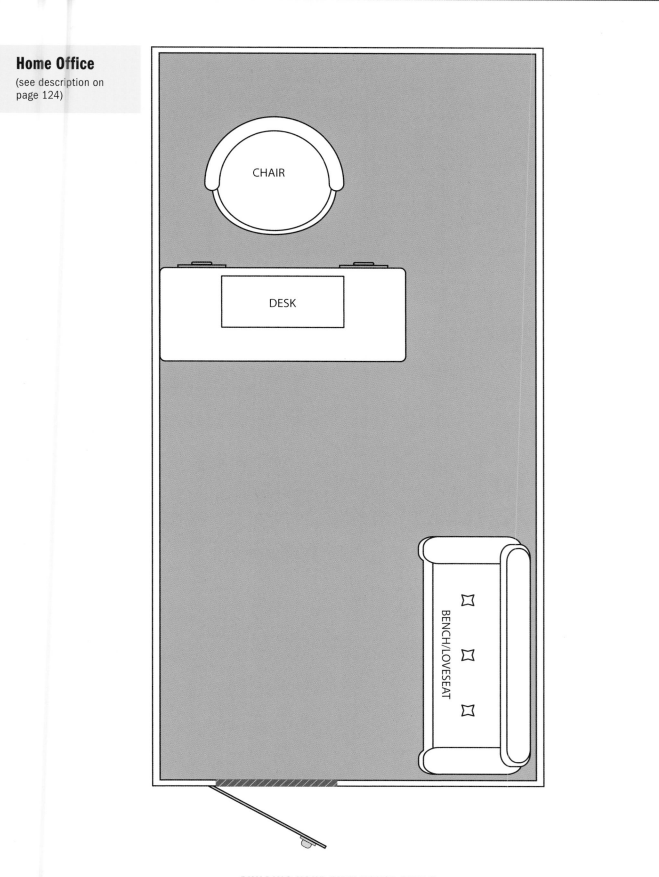

Home Office

(see description on
page 124)

CHAIR

DESK

BENCH/LOVESEAT

Pool House

(see description on page 125)

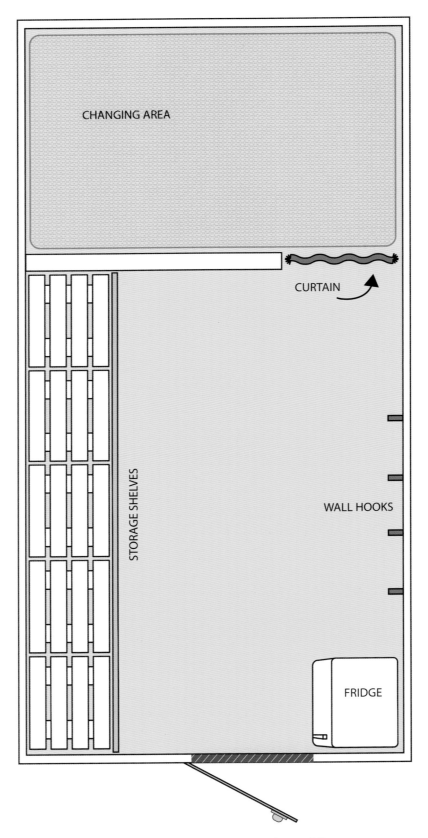

CHANGING AREA

CURTAIN

STORAGE SHELVES

WALL HOOKS

FRIDGE

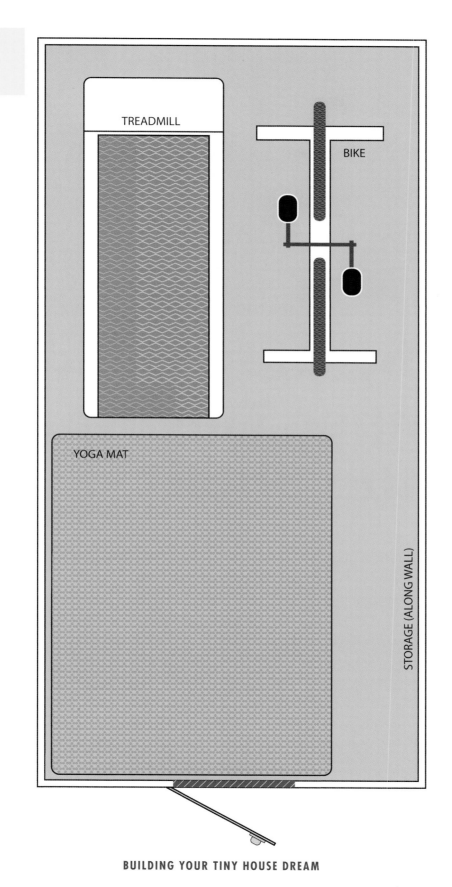

TREADMILL

BIKE

YOGA MAT

STORAGE (ALONG WALL)

NOW YOU HAVE A SHELL—DO YOUR OWN THING

Step-by-Step Building a Camper Tiny House from the Shell

Many of the scenarios and possible uses outlined in the previous section are rather stationary by nature, but not everyone will want that. Many people will want to travel with this build; after all, it's built on wheels. For the remainder of this instructional sequence, I am going to stay true to the original tiny house vision of a home that you can take with you wherever you go; I'll show you how to turn your tiny house shell into a camper tiny house. It will be an incredibly beautiful, custom camper, a far cry from the sometimes soulless manufactured campers out there.

Most manufactured campers have single-pane windows and are poorly insulated. They tend not to hold up very well over time and use. They are made of fiberglass and a variety of other synthetic materials. Many people have sensitivities to the various products and chemicals that are used for the manufacturing processes of these materials. As some of the materials age, they off-gas, which means that you are breathing in chemicals that could potentially be harmful to you.

Your "urban escape pod," as I often like to call this kind of build, is an excellent alternative to all of that. Your camper will have a level of comfort, coziness, and quality that you just won't find in a manufactured camper. So let's get going with the rest of the build, picking up from where we left off on page 123.

Camper Build Breakdown

Section	Materials (main)	Cost Estimate	Tools (main)	Time Estimate
Bed Area	2 sheets of ½" (1.3cm) plywood, 2x4s, adhesive, screws	$100	Jigsaw, miter saw, impact driver	8 hours
Kitchen Area	2x3s (4x), thin plywood, countertop, doors, hinges, sink, water storage, pump	$250	Impact driver, router, jigsaw	8 hours
Seating Area	½" (1.3cm) plywood, 2x4, hinges	$50	Impact driver, miter saw, jigsaw	5 hours
Storage	Cabinet, angle bracket	$100	Jigsaw, impact driver	5 hours
Back Windows	Bubble windows for pets (2x), silicone	$100	Circle cutter, jigsaw, impact driver	6 hours
More Visual Flair	Cedar trim, cedar plank (for planters), 2x4, plants and pots, silicone	$150	Table saw, impact driver, miter saw, air tool brad nailer	8 hours
TOTAL		$750		40 hours

NOTE: Cost of tools not included in pricing estimates. These are rough estimates; your timing and cost of materials may vary.

Bed Area

In this phase, we'll paint the interior, create a bed, and design an optional headboard.

1. Before we start installing the features of the inside of this house, let's get it painted. I painted the walls white and the ceiling a lovely seafoam green. Choose whatever colors suit your fancy. Follow the standard procedure you would when painting a room in a house. If you've never painted a room before, search the Internet for a tutorial; there are plenty out there. Use painter's tape (shown in this photo along the ceiling) to make sure you have crisp, clean paint lines on the areas you are painting. Before painting, I installed some pieces of plywood trim along the bottoms of the walls, covering up the vapor barrier that extends past the wood flooring (see step 132 on page 113 in the chapter Step-by-Step Building the Shell); here you can see it implemented, how the thin plywood very nicely and cleanly covers up the plastic liner and tape.

2. The walls have been fully painted. It's time to move to the ceiling. Those lights will have to move out of the way.

3. Pull the lights away from the ceiling plywood and paint all around the holes, as well as along the seams between the plywood pieces.

4. Finish painting the whole ceiling to your satisfaction.

5. Now it's time to tackle the bed. We need to build a platform for a mattress to rest on, which you can see in progress in this photo. We're working off a 5' x 10' (152.4 x 304.8cm) trailer, but the added width of the bump-outs means that the structure can comfortably house a mattress oriented perpendicular to the direction of travel (i.e., widthwise across the trailer, with the head against one side wall and the foot against the other side wall). You don't want the bed to sit on the floor parallel to the direction of travel, because that's not a good use of space.

A twin mattress is narrower than a full or a queen. If you're sure that you won't need space for two to sleep, then install a platform for a twin mattress; it will save a lot of floor space and living space. But if you're ever planning to sleep two in the camper, then a twin mattress won't really be suitable. For this particular build, I chose to go with a full-size mattress rather than a queen. A full-size mattress is 74½" (189.2cm) long and 53" (134.6cm) wide. Ensure that the platform you build is big enough to suit this size. In the case of this build, the length should simply be the entire width of the inside of the trailer from the left wall to the right wall, and the width should be the 53" (134.6cm) required to fit the mattress.

6. The platform itself is just a bare sheet of ½" (1.3cm) plywood, not painted and sealed like the plywood that we used for the front and back walls. Depending on the plywood thickness and the weight of the person or people sleeping on the bed, just the plywood alone could be sufficient, but over time, it will sag and warp, so it's always better to reinforce it. To do this, we'll be adding a supporting framework of 2x4s installed to the underside of the platform (see step 9 for an illustration of the entire framework). Make this framework using three 2x4s installed parallel to the orientation of the bed—that is, from head to foot. The first 2x4 should be flush with the side of the bed that will touch the front wall, and the other two should be roughly equidistant from that first 2x4, with a larger, unsupported span of plywood at the side of the bed that will face the interior of the space (visible in the photo for step 5).

Apply glue all along the 1½" (3.8cm) widths of the 2x4s and position them on the underside of the plywood, perpendicular to the plywood. Mark both ends of each 2x4 on the edge and top of the plywood and allow the glue to dry. Then flip the assembly over so the top side is up, and draw a straight line between the markings for each 2x4 (to follow the line of the 2x4). That is your guideline for screwing the 2x4s in place. Screw down through the plywood into these vertically mounted 2x4s.

7. Flip the whole assembly back upside down again. Now add more 2x4 pieces perpendicular to the ones that go from head to foot. These new pieces are where the bed will actually rest on the bump-outs, as you can see in this photo and in the photo for step 8. (In all of these photos, you can see these 2x4s resting on other 2x4s, which is discussed in step 9.) Measure in from the walls to figure out exactly where you need to place these 2x4s so that they will sit at the inner edge of the bump-outs, flush with the edge, as shown in the photos. Cut the 2x4s into pieces to perfectly fit in between each of the head-to-foot 2x4s you have already installed (this will be three pieces per end of the bed). Trace and mark as needed, and then glue and screw into place. This completes the supporting framework.

8. Here you can see the bed platform in place. Full disclosure: I had a lot of trouble maneuvering this bed platform once I got it inside the structure. I was unable to reposition it into its proper place. I ended up having to cut the front end of the platform off, right in front of the front-most (door side) head-to-foot 2x4, in order to maneuver it in two pieces separately. You can see in this photo where the cut is. These things happen; I'm not ashamed to admit it. Building is always going to have its twists and turns. You need to be able to adapt if and when necessary. And you may need to do exactly what I did if you're following this build very closely!

Supporting Framework

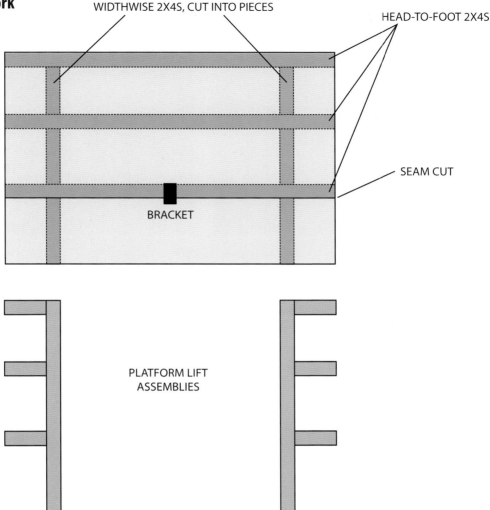

WIDTHWISE 2X4S, CUT INTO PIECES

HEAD-TO-FOOT 2X4S

SEAM CUT

BRACKET

PLATFORM LIFT ASSEMBLIES

9. You can also see in the previous photo, as mentioned earlier, that there are some additional 2x4s sitting underneath the widthwise 2x4s that were installed directly to the platform in pieces in step 7. These additional 2x4s are what we can call the platform lift assemblies. There is one on each end of the bed. These assemblies lift the bed platform off the ground a little bit higher and add precious storage space underneath the bed platform by doing so. Don't go too high, though, because then you could wind up blocking the window, depending on how thick your mattress is. Creating the platform lift assemblies is optional.

If you choose to do it, simply create an assembly that mirrors the supporting framework on each end of the bed (see the illustration for more detail). That means one long 2x4 with

three short 2x4 pieces installed perpendicularly to it. You can see one of these short perpendicular pieces in the background of the photo for step 12. This perpendicular configuration creates a stable base, which is essential because the platform lift assemblies are neither attached to the platform nor to the bump-outs—they simply sit in place, and the supporting framework under the bed platform sits on top of them. The bed platform itself can't go anywhere since it's up against the wall on the left and right sides and is pushed against the front wall. I chose not to bolt down the entire system because I wanted the build to be flexible in case I (or whoever uses it) decided to change to a smaller bed size later; by following my method here, you could easily cut down the entire assembly and change the full-size bed platform into a twin-size bed platform.

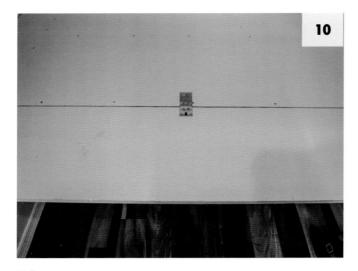

10. Here is a close-up of where I had to cut the bed platform into two pieces in order to maneuver it. Once the pieces were in place, I used a small bracket in the middle on the top and some small brackets to either side underneath to reattach the cut-off front section of the platform to the rest of the platform.

11. I also added a piece of 2x4 underneath the middle bracket to lend support and strength. If I hadn't added this, the bracket would have only been screwed into the plywood. Having a 2x4 directly below the bracket gives it more strength, since now the bracket is mounted not just into the plywood but also into this small section of 2x4.

12. The right angle of the foremost head-to-foot 2x4 and the pieces of 2x4 perpendicular to that create a pocket on the bump-out underneath the bed platform on each side. These are a great place to store towels, clothing, or whatever you want. You can still lift this entire platform to access things underneath, but it quickly becomes cumbersome and heavy, especially when you have a mattress on top of it; it's certainly more of a two-person job. Whenever possible, you'll want to just crawl under the bed to get what you need.

13. You can be done with your bed area now if you choose—the essentials are complete. However, you could also decide to add a headboard. I had a scrap of live-edge black walnut lying around, so I unleashed my creativity to turn it into a headboard. My vision for this headboard was to mount the piece of walnut on top of some copper piping. I'll walk you through what I did.

14. Drill holes into the bottom of the walnut to take the copper piping (do not drill the holes all the way through, just make pockets for the piping to fit into, about 1½" [3.8cm] deep). Make these holes all along the length of the walnut. Put construction adhesive into the bottom of the holes.

15. Then mount the copper tubes into the holes and let dry while the entire piece is still clamped or propped upside down. Here is the piece lying flat once the adhesive has dried. The copper pipe is standard ½" (1.3cm) pipe available at any hardware store. There is a fairly inexpensive pipe-cutting tool (a hand tool) you can use to cut the pieces to length. Using a bit of steel wool on the surface of the copper pipe also brings out a really beautiful shine while removing scratches or any printed-on barcodes that the pipe might have.

16. For extra security and strength, screw through the back of the headboard and into each copper tube. Make sure the screw length is just long enough to go in through the tube and out the other side into the front part of the wood, but not so long as to pierce through the front surface of the wood.

17. To make the walnut surface a little more agreeable and comfortable to use as a headboard and to lean against, you'll want to sand it. Start with something like an 80-grit sandpaper and work your way through finer and finer grits, finishing with a 400-grit sandpaper. The higher the grit number, the smoother the finish you'll achieve. Once it is as smooth as you want it, clean the dust off and apply a coat of linseed oil again. Note: Be careful with any rags or applicators you use to apply linseed oil. If left in a warm environment, linseed oil–coated materials can combust. Make sure you read the product instructions carefully for more information.

Now, here I made a bit of a mistake. I attached the headboard to the wall using one long screw that went right through the headboard into one of the wall framing 2x3s. (You can see it installed in the gallery on page 13.) Can you spot the mistake? I'll tell you: a few steps ago, I explained how the bed platform is liftable, but permanently installing this headboard makes it fairly unliftable, unless you want to take that screw out any time you need to lift it. By deciding to install a headboard, I negated some of the flexibility that I had originally designed in. Of course, that's not the end of the world, but in the interest of full disclosure, I wanted to point this out to you so that you can learn from my mistake.

Kitchen Area

This kitchen is minimal, and it doesn't include a fridge, but it does provide a cooking area and a sink. You can get ideas for how to include more appliances, like a fridge, starting on page 163.

18. Shown here is the left-hand side when you walk through the door, which is where we'll be installing a small kitchen area. When I say "kitchen," I mean essentially a countertop, sink, and a bit of storage. Underneath the countertop and sink, install an electric pump that draws water out of a multi-gallon reservoir, as well as a gray water tank for the sink drainage. An electrical outlet up near the top where the kitchen counter meets the wall makes it easy to hook up an electrical cooktop, but you could run an extension cord if you don't follow my electrical plan exactly. For more detail on setting up the guts of the sink workings, see the illustration on page 163.

STEP 18 CONTINUED ON PAGE 141

The low-voltage wire you see coming out of the wall is there to power an electric water pump for the kitchen sink. This is a great example of running electrical wire in the wall based on where you anticipate needing it for your final vision for your build. In this case, I knew where I was going to place the kitchen area, and I also knew that I wanted to incorporate an electric water pump for the sink. That planning led me to run the appropriate wiring to this place prior to completing the shell build and closing up the walls.

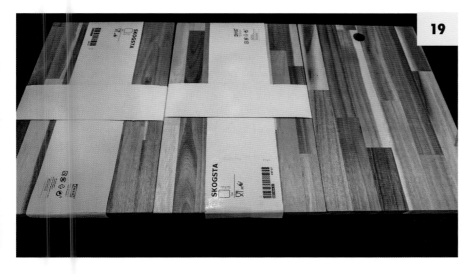

19. Many big box stores sell entire countertops, but they are usually 6' (182.9cm) or 8' (243.8cm) long, which is significantly more than we need here. So, I got creative again: I found three beautiful, rather large cutting boards at IKEA® and decided to put them together in a row to turn them into a countertop. These cutting boards happened to have a hole at the back of the board, but I wasn't too bothered by that, since you can always stick a serving implement into the hole.

20. Whatever you are using as a countertop, create a framework on the underside by screwing on a set of 2x3s. In my case, the framework does double duty of attaching the three cutting boards to one another to form the single countertop.

21. As you are measuring the 2x3s, use short scrap bits of 2x3s in the corners as placeholders for the upright legs that will be attached next. Screw the four 2x3s into place from the bottom of the 2x3s up into the countertop, but not all the way through—make sure your screws are just the right length. The long distance through a 2x3 is 2½" (6.4cm), so to go through the 2x3 and into the cutting board countertop, you need about 2¾" (7cm) screws. That creates the needed attachment without the screw ends coming up through the top of the kitchen counter.

22. Two of the legs need to be shorter than the others. The short legs are the back legs that will be set against the wall on top of the bump-out. The long legs are the front legs that will go all the way down to the floor. Take these measurements and cut the legs from 2x3s. Replace the scrap bits with the actual legs and screw them to the horizontal 2x3s installed in step 21, straight in from each side. Make sure not to screw the second screw into the first screw—one screw should go in slightly below the other.

23. After you've installed the basic framework attached to the countertop and the four legs, add additional braces using 2x3s as shown. This will make the entire kitchen assembly stronger and more stable. In total, you should add the following:

- Two horizontal braces (A) between the front and back legs that sit on top of the bump-out

- One horizontal brace (B) between the back legs that sits on top of the bump-out

- One horizontal brace (C) between the front legs that sits on the floor

- One horizontal brace (D) between the front legs that is positioned about 1' (30.5cm) off of the floor

- One vertical brace (E) between the 1' (30.5cm) horizontal brace (D) and the front horizontal 2x3 framework underneath the cabinet (not pictured here, but indicated with red lines)

The brace that "floats" at the front of the structure (D) is to delineate the bottom of the door area of the cabinet. This will be covered in step 26. The vertical brace (E) is visible in step 27, after the door holes have been cut. Decide on the exact placement of these two braces based on the size and shape of your door(s); see step 26.

Since you now have the entire structure of the kitchen cabinet created, you can push it completely into the corner of the structure. The left edge of the countertop should be touching the back wall of the tiny house, and the back edge of the countertop should line up with the side wall. Once in place, you can run four or five screws through the 2x3s into the bump-outs and/or into the bottom 2x3 that runs the length of the structure's side wall. This secures the structure in place.

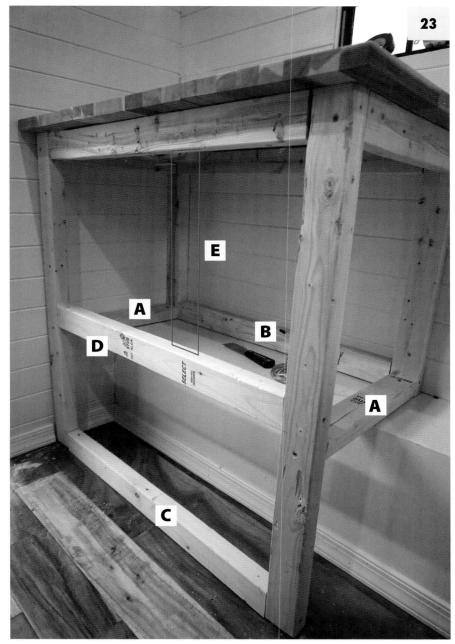

24. Cut a hole in the countertop to fit your sink. You can use whatever sink you want, but I'll explain how to install the kind of sink I chose. I used a stainless steel salad bowl as a sink. For a sink installation like this, the bowl needs to have a fairly formidable lip, at least ¼" (0.6cm). Trace the total circumference of the bowl (including the lip) on top of the countertop, and then draw another circle ¼" (0.6cm) (or however thick the lip on your bowl is) in from the first circle. The cut will be made on the inner line, allowing the bowl to sit in the hole and the lip to rest on the countertop, suspending the bowl in place.

Before you make the cut, put down some painter's tape all around the line you are going to cut. There are several reasons to do this. It will make it easier to see your line; it will protect the countertop from being scratched by the jigsaw; and it will also help prevent the cut edge from splintering and becoming ragged as the blade of the jigsaw pulls up and down. Drill a hole inside the lines to give your jigsaw blade a place to start, and make your cut.

25. Here you can see the bowl nestled neatly in the hole. Don't forget to cut a hole into the bottom of the sink for the drain. I used a drill and then a round file to expand the hole I drilled to the size I needed. This is also a good stage at which to cut the hole for and install the spigot into the countertop. You can more or less follow the instructions for installing the sink. This hole is also achieved by using a drill. The size of the hole will depend on what kind of faucet you are mounting (hand pump or electric pump faucets are recommended).

26. Now it's time to figure out the door placement, cover the front of the kitchen assembly with plywood, and cut the door holes. Each door will be attached by hinges, and those hinges need to be screwed to a vertical 2x3. In my case, I have a set of doors that meet in the middle, so the left door will be screwed to the left leg and the right door will be screwed to the right leg. The vertical brace (E) (see step 23) should sit right where the doors meet (and my doors are two different sizes). Cut a thin ¼" (0.6cm)–thick piece of plywood to the size and shape needed to cover the front of the assembly. The height of that piece will be the measurement from the flooring to the countertop, and the width will be from the extreme left side of the cabinet to the right corner edge. Measure and mark each of the doors on this piece of plywood (with it temporarily propped up against the framing), then measure, mark, and install the vertical brace (E) and the horizontal brace (D) in accordance with your door placement. Finally, use a compressor with brad finishing nails to attach the plywood to the framing.

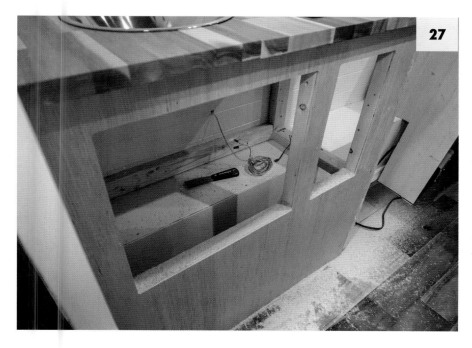

27. If you have a router with a bit with a ball bearing on the end (as used to cut the doorway in step 76 on page 88 in the chapter Step-by-Step Building the Shell), and have very precisely placed the vertical brace (E) and horizontal brace (D), you can simply use the router to follow that framing to cut the holes for the doors. If you haven't been that precise, haven't been able to be that precise because of the shapes/sizes of your door(s), or don't have the correct kind of bit, use a jigsaw to make the cuts.

28. For the side, cut out the plywood shape to accommodate the bump-out, and then install it. Then cover the corner edge all the way down the right front leg with a piece of angle trim so that it doesn't look raw and exposed. This side shot was taken before cutting the holes into the front for the doors, but you get the idea.

29. Here is the finished kitchen assembly with the cabinet doors installed. At this point, you can proceed to install the sink workings. Install an electric pump and water reservoir below the sink to feed up into the faucet and the tubes or piping leading to the gray water reservoir for wastewater from the sink.

Seating Area

Now let's move to the right side of the structure, directly across from the kitchen, to create a seating area with some hidden storage.

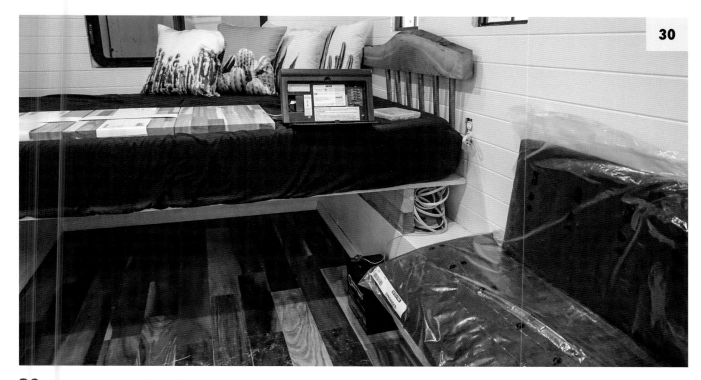

30. The bump-out lends itself nicely to creating a seating area because you already have that raised surface, which can act like a bench. Purchase a cushion for the seat as well as a cushion to install on the wall to lean against while sitting on the seat. Mine came from IKEA®.

31. To make the bench seat more comfortable for the average sitter as well as to create storage space underneath it, we're going to raise it up off the bump-out using 2x4s. Measure the length and width of your seat cushion. Cut four short sections of 2x4s, with 45-degree angles on the ends; the longest side (along the top) should be a little bit shy of the width of your seat cushion. Mount them vertically as shown, with the piece on each end sitting a few inches shy of the length of your seat cushion (rather than flush with the edge of the seat cushion). Screw straight down through them into (but not through) the bump-out below.

32. Measure and cut a piece of ½" (1.3cm)–thick or ¾" (1.9cm)–thick plywood to the exact dimensions of your seat cushion and paint it the desired color. Cut a narrow piece of this piece, about 2½" (6.4cm) wide, and screw it along the back of the 2x4s, flush against the wall. This will be the back part of the seat that the front part of the seat will attach to with hinges. Such a setup will allow for the seat to lift up, revealing the storage space underneath.

33. Install three more short pieces of 2x4s in between each of the four existing 2x4s, flush with the edge of the bump-out. This creates three little pockets underneath the bench, which are fantastic for storing small things. The three short pieces you just installed ensure that while you are towing, nothing can slide out of the pockets. If you prefer to leave one of the three pockets open in order to slide something larger into the space, such as an extra blanket, you can, but just remember to move the item(s) before towing.

34. Take the remaining piece of painted plywood and use two sets of long hinges to attach it to the thin strip of plywood. It's a cinch to lift the hinged bench platform to access the storage space beneath. (In this photo, the hinges haven't been installed yet.)

35. Place the seat cushion on top of your assembly, but leave it covered in plastic for now so that it doesn't get dirty as you complete your build. There is no need to permanently install this cushion—it should sit pressed against the right wall, and it will need to be able to shift whenever you lift up the hinged bench platform.

36. Install the back cushion when you're sure you won't dirty it with further construction (or install it now and cover it up with fabric or plastic). To mount it to the wall, I used two screws and a fancy brass washer, which makes the mounting points look more elegant, like two buttons.

37. To the left side of the bench seat, between the seat and the head of the bed, there is small space that is perfect for an essential electrical component: the electrical panel. As explained in the electrical section, all of the wires in the house should converge in this electrical panel, including the 110V AC wiring and the 12V DC wiring (used for the LEDs in the ceiling, for example). For this build, I located the panel on the side of the bed platform to create a kind of bedside table. More often than not, though, I tuck the entire electrical assembly underneath the bed platform. For this build, I installed the panel between some scrap pieces of wood to secure it and help it blend into the rest of the interior.

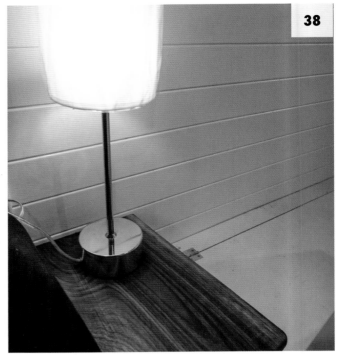

38. Add a "nightstand" above the electrical panel. I had a lovely piece of black walnut to use, but you can use any kind of wood. Improvise with what you have, simply adding some vertical supports underneath your top and screwing everything in place.

39. This is also a good time to install the backup battery in the front right corner, under the bed. Mount this to the floor between some pieces of wood so that it can't shift around. See more detail about it in the electrical section on page 103.

Storage

The last installation or "piece of furniture" to make inside the tiny house is a small storage cabinet that fits in between the kitchen and the bed. In these photos, the kitchen hasn't been permanently installed yet, so you can see more clearly around the work being done.

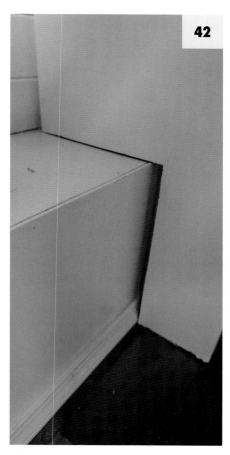

40. Here's a trick you can whip out whenever you have a chance: adapt an existing piece to suit your needs. Like the cutting boards we used for the kitchen countertop, this storage unit is made from a store-bought (IKEA®) shelving unit that has been customized to fit the space.

41. Before you purchase a unit to customize, make sure that it is not too wide to fit the space you have for it, and that it won't obstruct anything on the wall, like this electrical outlet.

42. After assembling the shelving unit according to the manufacturer's instructions, cut off the bottom of the unit in order to lower the shelves to a height of just below the side windows. Then cut out a cubic rectangle from the entire back of the unit so that the unit can sit neatly on the bump-out.

43. It's pretty easy to cut out the sections—you can see them here. I personally like a lot of IKEA's products, since they tend to be quite versatile, look stylish, and, for the most part, hold up reasonably well. As an added bonus, if you change your mind about a piece later, you can quickly and easily remove it and replace it with a new custom piece without spending a ton of money (or time).

44. Mount the customized unit to one of the vertical 2x3s behind the tongue-and-groove pine wall covering (one of the 2x3s that forms the wall framing). I use a small angle bracket to achieve this. This firmly locks the unit in place. Then fill out the shelves as desired. I placed a cloth storage cube in the top section; when traveling, I take it out and put it onto the bed platform so that it doesn't fly around. In the smaller bottom section, I opted to put in a metal cage-like add-on, perfect for documents and a couple of books.

Back Windows

It's time to add some impressively stylish circular bubble windows to the back of the house, including the door. Now, I could have added these earlier in the construction process, but I simply didn't, so I'm going to teach you how to do it now, the way I did. In order to add these windows, we need to create circular cutouts all the way through the back walls and door. (The door is essentially done the same way as the walls, so I'll refer to the walls only for the remainder of these instructions.) Making these circular cutouts is more difficult now that the interior walls have already been covered with the finishing pine boards, but it's still completely achievable.

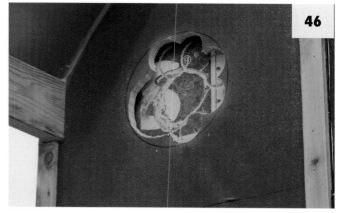

45. The bubble windows have a flat lip all the way around, through which you drive screws to attach the window. Trace the window onto the exterior plywood. Measure the width of the lip on the window. Then trace a second circle on the inside of the first, exactly the width of the lip smaller. Like you did for the sink installation, you'll be cutting this interior circle to make the window hole. (Alternatively, use a compass to draw a circle the exact diameter of the opening of the window.)

To make the window cutting process a little easier, use a circle cutter to cut through the outer plywood. Simply cut seven small circles in the plywood all along the inner edge of the full circle you have outlined. In between the plywood and the interior pine, there is a layer of foam board insulation, which we'll deal with later.

46. Repeat on the other side as well for the second back window. (I did so rather inelegantly, as you can see by this blobby cutout.)

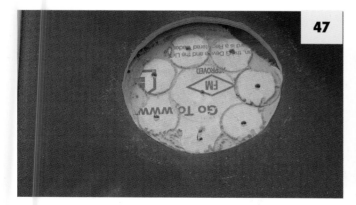

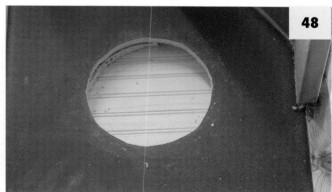

47. Next, use a router to finalize the full circular cutout. Be very careful, though, since these windows do not have interior framing. The router can cut more than you want if you don't have a very steady hand. I suggest using an oscillating tool to finalize this cutout as a safer alternative that is less prone to error.

48. Now we need to get to the inner pine. Strip away the insulation within the hole to expose the backside of the pine. You can use a utility knife for this or chip away at the foam insulation with a chisel. Either way, the material is pretty easy to manipulate into the cutout you want.

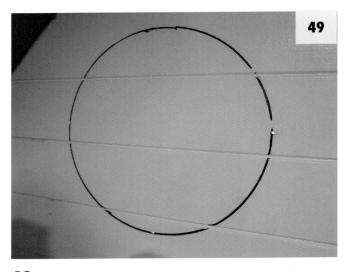

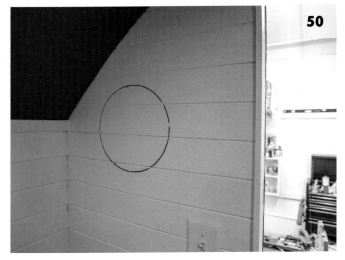

49. From the outside, send four pilot holes through the pine, evenly spaced around the inner edge of the circle cutout. Then, on the inside wall, use a compass (or string and pen) to connect the pilot holes into a complete circle outline.

50. In this photo you can see a little better the placement of the window. Make sure your placement works for you both inside and outside the house.

51. Go ahead and cut through the pine just like you cut through the exterior plywood. Your hole is complete. Now pop in the windows. Where the window lip meets the exterior wall, add a sealant, since this is a potential water intrusion point. You will also have an open space in between the exterior plywood wall and the interior pine wall. I closed up that space with a thin piece of flexible vinyl (harvested from a vertical slat in a slatted window blind). Any flexible material cut to the right thickness and length will do. Using vinyl instead of something like cardboard or similar will certainly yield more longevity, though. You can see the clean look this achieves in some of the gallery photos on pages 11–12. The window in the door is not as critical to finish in this way, since the door is thinner and doesn't create an ugly gap like the wall structure does.

More Visual Flair

It's time for the finishing touches: trim, planters, and extra details that will make this build really eye-catching and feel personalized from the inside out.

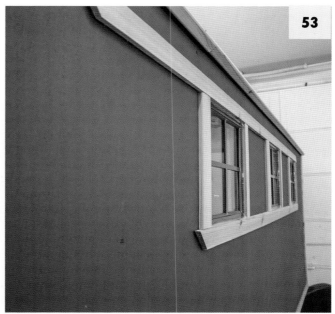

53. Around the windows, use short strips for the sides and long strips with stylish angled edges along the top and bottom.

52. I put some nice cedar trim all around the outside of the house, including around the door. Cedar is a good choice because it doesn't need to be treated before being exposed to the elements; it's very robust and will naturally gray over time in the sun as it weathers. This is the same cedar trim used around the side windows way back in step 127 on page 110 in the chapter Step-by-Step Building the Shell. Use a table saw to cut the trim into thin strips. Surround the exterior horizontally all along the bottom and top edges, and also fill in the corners. Seal underneath each piece with silicone sealant as described in step 128 on page 111 in the chapter Step-by-Step Building the Shell, and use a compression finish nailer to affix the pieces into place. Around the door, leave a small cutout for the door ledge to slot into whenever you open the door.

54. Anywhere there's an edge, or a place where two pieces of plywood meet, is generally not visually appealing, so add cedar trim.

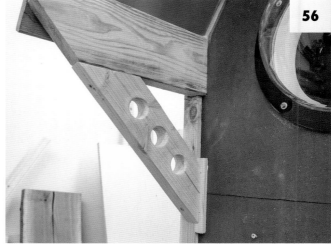

55. At the back (door) end of the house, add an angular 2x6 brace extending from the 45-degree angle of the end of each 2x6 roofing beam. This is in part for additional support, but it also adds a beautiful visual element to the back of the home. Cut three circular holes into each brace for some real flair. If you're good at painting flowers or leafy vines, you could do that as well. I'm not that good at that, so I stuck with drilling holes.

56. Here's the other side, where you can clearly see that I had to add a bit of extra wood to the inside to make a solid base for each brace. The braces themselves are mounted with a screw through the tapering edge into the 2x6 roofing beam and into the corner where the side wall and back wall meet.

57. Speaking of flair, why not create some cute planters under the windows? This is very easy to do. Take a length of cedar board. Cut a piece for the flat top and two angled braces for the supports underneath. These holders can be mounted with a simple metal 90-degree angle bracket, one end mounted into the planter and one into the back wall of the house. Using a circle cutter, cut holes for the flowerpots in the flat top. Make sure your pots are wider at the top than the bottom; that way, you can easily pop them in and out, no other fastening required. Take the flowerpots out while traveling, since it's not good for the plants and you might lose a pot or two on a bump in the road.

58. The seating area table is a suitably sized piece of live-edge wood that is mounted to a table mount designed for boats. Search "flush mount boating table" on eBay or Amazon to see examples of these. On such a mount, there is an aluminum cup with a lip on it. That cup is dropped into an appropriately sized hole that you cut into the floor with a circle cutter. There are a few screw holes to secure the cup to the floor. There is another receptacle at the other end that attaches to the bottom of the tabletop (more of a surface mount than a recessed one like the floor mount). I like that this allows me to use any tabletop I choose and not be married to some vinyl tabletop that wouldn't pair up well with the rest of the look and feel of the interior of the tiny house.

59. An approximately 2½" (6.4cm)–thick hollow metal pipe connects the floor cup (shown in this photo) to the tabletop cup. Nothing gets permanently attached together, since the pipe is just held in place by the cups under the tabletop and the cup in the floor. Therefore, you can always pull up on the table and it will detach from the floor. This is good to do when you are traveling, since the table could jostle itself loose and do damage to the floor or the rest of the interior. You can also remove the table if you need a bit more floor space for some reason. The recessed cup in the floor doesn't create any hurdles or trip hazards. This kind of mount is a pretty versatile solution, and I like using them in my builds.

60. Everything in this section, and this chapter—indeed, basically everything in this entire build—you can copy exactly if you want, or you can simply look at what I did for inspiration to do your own thing. The reality is that you may not have access to some of the specific materials I used, or you may not like how I finished certain aspects of the build. That's all fine—do what you like. The real prize is creating something for your own use. So, what are you going to build?

Adding a Kitchen and Bathroom

Let's spend a bit more time talking about kitchens and bathrooms. This book's build is a very small 50-square-foot (4.6-square-meter) structure, and tiny houses are a collection of compromises. You have to weigh very carefully what's important to you. And if you want to use one of these structures as a full-time residence, there are certain things it has to have: some form of bathroom and some kind of kitchen. In this chapter, we'll outline what your options are and get you thinking about what's important to you. You'll need to decide for yourself what approach to take for putting a kitchen and bathroom into this structure. We're going to use the home of Emily and Dan, who you met on page 45, as an example. They live full time in a customized version of this build.

Before we get started, here's a heads-up: If you're building a structure the size of what is outlined in this book, you're not going to have a dishwasher. You're not going to have a washing machine. You're not going to have a bathtub. Put them out of your mind from the start and focus on the other elements that really matter.

There's a kitchen and bathroom in here somewhere.

Bathroom

Toilet

Let's start with the obvious: the toilet. For a small structure like this, an **RV toilet (or "camping toilet")** is a viable solution. It is a small, boxy-looking chemical toilet that flushes by way of a pump mechanism. You use the toilet in the same way that you would a regular toilet. When you go to flush, you use a pump mechanism (either hand-powered or electric) that flushes everything into a holding tank. The flushing water comes from a reservoir tank that is integrated into the toilet itself. There is an indicator on the holding tank that tells you when the tank is full. The liquid in the holding tank is like the blue chemical stuff you see on planes sometimes; it's very effective at eliminating odors and breaking down materials. At some point, though, you will need to empty the toilet, and for that, you will need a place to do so in a safe and environmentally friendly manner. Typically, you can simply dispose of your waste into a regular flush toilet. Campgrounds, RV parks, and some rest areas offer dump stations where the contents of an RV toilet can be disposed of, too. RV toilets are made to be used with a particular kind of toilet paper that is designed to dissolve and break down better and faster than regular toilet paper.

The tiny house world has also really embraced **composting toilets**, because they're straightforward to incorporate in a small space. A composting toilet can be as simple as a bucket with a toilet seat. To use it, you lay down a layer of sawdust or other absorbent material. Then, after you do your business, you lay down another layer of the absorption material over the previous layer. This wicks out any moisture, and the result fosters the composting process. Although these units are called composting toilets, the "composting" does not actually take place inside the toilet itself. Composting is a slow breakdown of organic materials and requires time to take place. To facilitate the process, a composting bin of some kind will need to be available or constructed as an add-on component to the toilet. There are a lot of ways to accomplish this; whole books have been written on this subject. There is also a wealth of information online about composting options, so do more research if you think you want to go this route. You can also do your business in a composting toilet setup but then simply discard the contents rather than composting it, which is what Emily and Dan do—this is called a dry toilet.

An RV toilet is self-contained and highly portable.

A bucket like this one can act as the simplest form of composting or dry toilet, and it's perfectly hygienic.

This basic homemade composting toilet has the sawdust ready to go.

A bucket is the simplest form of composting toilet, but some companies have produced rather elaborate and expensive composting toilets; they tend to be larger, so you may have to get creative in fitting one into this small house, but it's technically possible. Nature's Head is one of the more popular ones in the tiny house scene. A Nature's Head composting toilet is special because it has a couple of technical features that a simple bucket does not have. One of these features is a urine diverter: when you sit on the toilet, your urine and fecal matter are separated. This helps keep moisture down and aids in the composting process. Another feature is a churning mechanism: by utilizing a hand crank, you can mix everything and accelerate the composting process. Even if you are opting for a simple bucket method, it is still advisable to create a urine diverter. This can be a funnel that channels urine away into a separate holding container. Separating the urine will reduce smell and aid in the drying-out process that fecal matter undergoes with the sawdust.

There's also a toilet called a **dry flush toilet**. This toilet uses an external low-voltage power source, which could be run with a solar panel setup. Dry flush toilets utilize a cartridge system.

For the parents out there, if you're familiar with a device called the Diaper Genie, a dry flush toilet is very similar to that. You use the toilet, you hit the flush button, and a plastic sleeve envelops and compartmentalizes what's in the bowl. It pulls the air out of it, wraps it, and then resets itself to be used again. All you need to do is dispose of the sleeves. This is simple to do, since, much like baby diapers, when the waste is contained in the sealed plastic sleeve, it is fine to place in standard municipal/landfill-bound waste. The flush cartridges are relatively expensive unless you buy them in bulk (they will cost roughly $1 per flush); and if you're living in such a small space, there's not much you can buy in bulk. But depending on your needs, this could be an option for you.

What isn't an option is your typical standard flush toilet found in a regular residence. You may have an adequate water supply for other needs in your tiny house, but a flush toilet produces several gallons (many liters) of waste every time you flush. That all has to go somewhere. Unless you're connected to a septic system, or you can connect your house up to a standard sewer line, a regular flush toilet is out of the question. In addition, flush toilets are usually

A dry flush toilet, albeit a larger model than you would probably install in this small space.

when they're standing outside their tiny house, they reach back in through the window and control the water flow on the kitchen faucet. They adjust the temperature of the water and take their **shower right there on the outside of their home**. They have a shower curtain that they hook onto the side of the house to give them some privacy. This kind of shower is of course not a permanent attachment; once they're done showering, they simply take down the curtain and remove the handheld showerhead from the faucet. If you use this kind of setup, make sure to use only environmentally friendly soap.

made of porcelain, they're heavy, they can't be moved around, and they take up a lot of space—not great in 50 square feet (4.6 square meters).

There you have it: your toilet options. Emily and Dan use a simple composting toilet, and that works for them. Think about what will work for you.

Shower

The other component of a bathroom typically is a shower. A shower takes up a lot of space. I have a 2' x 2' (61 x 61cm) shower in my tiny house, and that's a very small shower; a 3' x 3' (91.4 x 91.4cm) stall is more of a standard size stall. However, 3' x 3' is 9 square feet (0.8 square meters), so we're talking about almost 20 percent of your floor space right there. It's simply not an option for a space of this size.

So what do Emily and Dan do for a shower? They have a very ingenious solution. They have a kitchen sink with a faucet. The faucet is connected to a water supply, and that water supply runs through a water heater and directly into that faucet, giving them both hot and cold water. What they do is connect a handheld showerhead to that kitchen faucet and run it out through one of their windows. Then,

A 2' x 2' (61 x 61cm) shower with adult male (me) for scale. There's not much wiggle room.

Compared to the 2' x 2' (61 x 61cm) shower, a 2½' x 3½' (76 x 107cm) shower is spacious—but you'll have trouble fitting it into your build.

Emily and Dan live in Georgia, where the weather for at least most of the year tends to be reasonably warm; having an exterior shower like theirs only ever makes sense in a place that enjoys a more temperate climate. Up north, where I have my tiny house in the Catskills region of New York, it's cold for a lot of the year, and I would not want to shower outside for the majority of the months before and after July and August. But everyone has their own limits; plenty of people swim in the ocean during cold months, and this isn't much different, especially if a heated interior is waiting for you just steps away.

My house covered in snow. I don't want to shower in this.

This exterior shower option is effectively your only option to integrate a shower into a small space like this. I've never met or heard of anyone with an interior shower in a space this small. That said, some people live in tiny houses **without any shower option**. They are mostly nomadic types who rely on other sources for their showers. There are a couple of ways you can go about it. Most truck stops will offer showers for a fee. But a popular solution is to purchase a gym membership to one of the larger chains in the country, like Retro Fitness, Blink, or Crunch. These chains have hundreds, if not thousands, of locations in the United States, and what the tiny house dwellers do is plan their travel around these gym locations. The gyms have a full locker room, bathroom, and shower setup. So they're not members of the gym in order to work out there—they are members of the gym in order to clean up, shower, and shave there. Then they're on their way again.

What it comes down to is what's feasible for you, where your house is going to be parked, what the weather is like in your area, and what you are ultimately comfortable with.

Emily and Dan's shower hookup, ready to stretch out the window.

Kitchen

Sink and (Hot) Water

When I put a kitchen space into a small structure like this, the kitchen typically includes a countertop of 4 to 6 square feet (0.4 to 0.6 square meters), depending on how important cooking is to the end user. Part of that counter is taken up by a **sink**. A metal salad bowl with a lip can work great as a sink, as we saw in the building instructions on page 144. You can go with my solution or buy a bigger or more elaborate sink; it's up to you.

When I consider water for a small structure like this, I typically will use a little **water reservoir**. I've utilized both 3- and 5-gallon (11.3 and 18.9L) reservoirs in the past. It's just a simple tank that sits inside the kitchen cabinet and that can be refilled. A tube leads from the tank up to some form of a faucet. The **faucet** is one of two types. In a manual pump faucet, you manually move a lever back and forth to cause a diaphragm to go back and forth inside the faucet, pulling the water up out of the tank. There is also a faucet that utilizes a small electric motor pump. There's an on/off switch on the faucet; you flip the switch on, and it pulls the water out of the tank by way of a low-voltage pump.

One of my standard salad-bowl-sink setups, with a manual pump faucet.

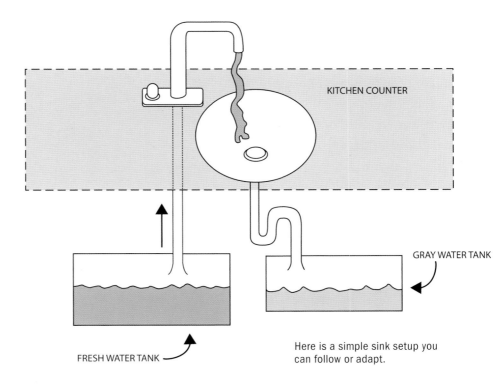

KITCHEN COUNTER

GRAY WATER TANK

FRESH WATER TANK

Here is a simple sink setup you can follow or adapt.

Water will emit from the faucet as long as that switch is turned on. Both of these kinds of faucets only provide cold water, though, and would not suit for a warm shower setup like the kind Emily and Dan have (see page 162).

If you want to set up your kitchen with both cold and hot water, similar to what Emily and Dan did, you will need a **water input point on the exterior of the tiny house**—essentially an RV water hookup. You hook a garden hose up to it. (This presupposes that you have some form of water source wherever your tiny house is located.) After the water enters the house, it splits into two lines. One line runs straight to the sink (the cold water line), and another line runs into a **water heater** and then into the sink from there. Emily and Dan have an electric 2.5-gallon (9.5L) water heater in their house. That means that at any given point, the water heater contains 2.5 gallons (9.5L) of hot water, ready to be used. When you start to draw water out of that tank, that water replenishes with cold water, and the heating process starts over. The downside to this is that the heating does not occur instantly in an on-demand fashion. Once the tank is depleted, it will take fifteen minutes or so for there to be another 2.5 gallons (9.5L) of hot water available for use.

Emily and Dan have both an electric hookup and a water supply where their house is parked, so none of this is an issue for them. One way you can forego the electricity requirement, though, is to utilize an on-demand propane heater. Such a heater would typically be mounted on the exterior of the house. The concept is the same: the water enters that propane heater when you turn on your hot water faucet. As the water flows through the heater, it triggers the ignition switch. That ignition switch lights a fire in a combustion chamber fueled

In this photo you can see the not-so-sneaky sink drainage in Emily and Dan's build.

On the right is a water input point. You can hook a garden hose up to this to provide water to a tiny home.

by propane. The flame heats a coil that the water is passing through. That water then exits the water heater and comes out of your faucet nice and hot. In contrast to an electric water heater, a propane heater creates hot water instantly, meaning you will continue to have hot water as long as you have water and propane. So if you like to take long, hot showers, you're probably better off with the propane option. It was quite genius of Emily and Dan to hook up a handheld showerhead to the kitchen faucet so they could get double the use out of their hot water system. They found a solution that works for them and within the confines of the space they have.

Cooking and Countertops

A kitchen is not only made up of a sink and faucet. I mentioned the countertop earlier; since there's so little space in a build this size, I would generally not go for a cooktop that is permanently mounted into the countertop. Instead, it makes more sense to have one that can be put away somewhere and brought out only when needed.

My favorite way of cooking in a tiny house is with an **induction cooktop**. There are a couple of reasons for this. First off, induction cooktops are electric, and my tiny house up in the Catskills runs entirely off of electric, so they are easy for me to use. The second great thing about induction cooktops is that they do not produce any heat. The induction process agitates the contents of the pot or pan that you have on top of the cooktop, but not the pot or pan itself, similar to what happens in a microwave. If you've ever put a cup of water into a microwave, you'll know that the water is what heats up, not so much the cup itself. So why is this good? We're all familiar with the old-fashioned electric coil cooking elements. Those heat up to the point where they are glowing hot; they produce a lot of heat, and the temperature in the small space of a tiny house

This tiny house, built by Trekker Trailers, has a propane tank and tub mounted to the hitch and a water heater mounted to the front wall, ensuring endlessly hot showers.

will go way up. That may be great if you're located somewhere cold—you can heat the house very quickly and effectively with that. But it's not good if you are somewhere warm, because the temperature in the house will become unbearable pretty quickly.

Many induction cooktops are thin and highly portable, allowing you to pull them out when you need them and put them away when you're done.

Induction cooktops come in various shapes and sizes. For a space this size, a single-burner induction cooktop is sufficient. That is all I have in my tiny house. If I'm making pasta, I'll cook the pasta, drain the water, pour the sauce into the same pot that I cooked the pasta in, and heat the sauce with the pasta. You just have to re-think the way you do certain things when you only have a single cooktop.

As you can see, it's entirely possible to cook inside your tiny house. However, whenever possible and feasible, I suggest you **cook outdoors**. Aside from all the heat you create in the house while cooking, humidity and ventilation are another concern. If you're cooking something like pasta, you're boiling water for ten minutes and creating a lot of steam. That steam is moisture, which can saturate such a small space very quickly. That can lead to an uncomfortable interior environment in the house. It also helps mold get a foothold in your home, and you don't want that.

There is a simple and elegant solution for cooking outdoors with this particular tiny house build. You can install a **wooden shelf** that folds down on the exterior of the house. You can place a camping stove on top of that. Cover the stove when it's raining, bring it inside when you're towing, and do your cooking out in the fresh air. It's really that simple and elegant. This is Emily and Dan's solution in their tiny home.

These are some of the options that are available to you when it comes time to cook. You can also consider adding other appliances based on what you like. You can have a blender if you want. I suggest keeping it small, like the Magic Bullet blenders. Another alternative to an induction cooktop is an Instant Pot®. There are a ton of things, and meals,

Slow cookers might seem like a great solution, but they actually produce a problematic amount of humidity in a tiny house.

Emily and Dan's camping stove sits on a wooden shelf that folds down on the exterior of the house.

you can cook easily and quickly in an Instant Pot. It's a fantastic tiny house appliance, and it tends to be very popular in the tiny house community.

Refrigerator

The biggest appliance that most kitchens typically have is the fridge. You have a range of options here. One of Emily and Dan's favorite things about living in such a small space is that it encourages them to seek out local sources of food, since they don't have ample storage in the refrigerator or on shelves. Tiny living promotes buying fresh food, and it forces you to buy smaller quantities and utilize them almost immediately. When you have a more substantial standard-size fridge, you may often buy too much at the supermarket, forget about it, not do any meal planning, and wind up wasting a lot of food. Emily and Dan have a small fridge inside their home, but when they are not connected to exterior power, they rely on a cooler for storing their fresh purchases, and those get used up very quickly.

There are a lot of **low-voltage fridge** options. They start at a very small level, which is intended to be a desktop fridge. These can be so small that they can't accommodate more than a six-pack of cans. Fridges continue to get bigger and bigger from there, and your choice of fridge is going to come down to whatever size best suits your needs. Low-voltage fridges also have the benefit of being powered from a solar panel setup, which could be an advantage if you do not have access to a dedicated power source.

Emily and Dan's fridge. You can pack just enough in there!

Conclusion: What's Next?

Regardless of what you have decided to build based on your own personal needs, take a moment to step back and see how far you've come. Whether you have actually already built something or not is irrelevant. The point is that you are now further along than you were before, and that's progress and forward momentum toward a goal. We all have to start somewhere. Just by reading this book, you are now better equipped to take on the project of creating your own living space. I encourage you to use that forward momentum and build on it in both a figurative and a literal sense. Have it be about you. Let it be empowering. Do it to affirm something for yourself and to show yourself what you are capable of.

Through my company, Tiny Industrial, I build these structures for other people because it fills me with a great amount of joy to be able to do so. It's my hope that this same feeling is what you get when tackling this kind of project. I also want you to understand that you are not alone in this process. Many people have done it, and they are a lot like you. Those people, including myself, are out there to help you in this process, and we form a very tight-knit tiny house community of people who come

from all different walks of life but who nevertheless share a very strong common bond and connection.

In two months, I'm heading to someone's wedding that I met through this great community. I'm also entering a joint business venture with another person in the tiny dwelling realm. My point is that there is a broader community of people building these structures out there that you can (if you want) be a part of, much in the same way that you would invariably meet new people if you took up a new sport of some kind. Use that connection. Reach out. Ask questions. In this space, people generally enjoy helping others. There is a lot of knowledge out there. Find the people who have it.

The other thing that I encourage you to do is to keep moving forward. That doesn't have to mean that you go out and buy the trailer foundation for your tiny house tomorrow. It could be something as simple as sketching out your own interior space layouts. It could be pondering what color you want your build to be. All of those kinds of things will enhance the likelihood of you actually doing it versus simply putting this book down and saying, "One day…"

When you do start down this path, involve others. It seems to me that we cocoon ourselves these days. Tell others of your plans. See if they want to help you on a financial, labor, or expertise level. Put it out there on your social media. It doesn't matter how you get people involved, but it's great to have other people invested in the outcome as well. All you have to do is mention to them that you are looking to

build a tiny house. There is no way that they will not be, at a minimum, intrigued. If there is one thing that I have found to be true, it is that the reaction I get when I tell people that I build tiny houses is always overwhelmingly positive. "Oh wow! That's so cool! I love tiny houses!" is a common response. There is no reason to believe that you wouldn't get the same response if you announce your desire to build one of these to the folks around you.

Make it happen. You got this! Best of luck to you in all your tiny house endeavors. When you build your first home (or second or third!), send me a picture at book@tinyindustrial.com.

Building Checklist

	PLANNING
	I know why I want to go tiny
	I'm ready at this point in my life to go tiny
	I can handle downsizing stuff as much as will be required to go tiny
	I have a clear vision of what tiny living looks like for me
	I have a timeline for when and how I want to go tiny
	I know what features my tiny house should have and what it should look like
	I have attended a tiny house show or building event to experience tiny houses up close
	I have a grasp on how much I will be moving my tiny house around
	I have familiarized myself with local rules and regulations regarding tiny houses
	I have a plan for how many windows there should be and where they should go
	I know how I'm going to finance the house
	I have access to the other resources I will need to build the house

BUILDING YOUR TINY HOUSE DREAM

	BUILDING
	I have access to the tools I'll need to build the house
	I have found a supplier for the kind of trailer I'll need for the build
	I'm comfortable using the tools that will be needed to do the work
	I'm physically able to do the work, such as lifting and carrying, that will be required for the build
	I have a place where I can build the house
	I realize that the house that this book will help me build will be very small
	I have a vehicle, or access to a vehicle, that I can use to move around the materials I need
	I feel comfortable installing all the systems that the house will need
	I'm bringing a level of self-confidence to the project that doesn't sacrifice my personal safety
	I can find people willing to help me complete the parts of the build I don't feel comfortable doing myself
	LIVING TINY
	I have done my research and know where and how I will live in my house legally
	I understand how to move/tow the tiny house safely
	I'm open to finding out things about myself that perhaps I wasn't aware of
	I know that some things will be more difficult in a tiny house
	I see more benefits than downsides to living tiny

Resources

Legalities/Informational

www.americantinyhouseassociation.org
www.unitedtinyhouse.com

Blogs

www.tinyhousetalk.com
www.tinyhouseexpedition.com
www.tinyhousegiantjourney.com
www.tinyhouseblog.com
www.relaxshacks.com
www.livingbiginatinyhouse.com

Plans

www.tinyhousedesign.com
www.tinyhouseplans.com
www.padtinyhouses.com

Inspiration

www.reddit.com/r/TinyHouses
www.tinyhousesandbeyond.com
www.tinyhouselistings.com

Shameless Plugs

www.tinyindustrial.com
www.tinyhouseinthecountry.com

Books

Diedricksen, Derek "Deek." *Humble Homes, Simple Shacks, Cozy Cottages, Ramshackle Retreats, Funky Forts: And Whatever the Heck Else We Could Squeeze in Here.* Lanham, MD: Lyons Press, 2012.

Diedricksen, Derek "Deek." *Micro Living: 40 Innovative Tiny Houses Equipped for Full-Time Living, in 400 Square Feet or Less.* North Adams, MA: Storey Publishing, 2018.

Diedricksen, Derek "Deek." *Microshelters: 59 Creative Cabins, Tiny Houses, Tree Houses, and Other Small Structures.* North Adams, MA: Storey Publishing, 2015.

Schapdick, Chris. *The Joy of Tiny House Living: Everything You Need to Know Before Taking the Plunge.* Mount Joy, PA: Fox Chapel Publishing, 2019.

Shafer, Jay. *Jay Shafer's DIY Book of Backyard Sheds & Tiny Houses: Build Your Own Guest Cottage, Writing Studio, Home Office, Craft Workshop, or Personal Retreat.* East Petersburg, PA: Fox Chapel Publishing, 2013.

Shafer, Jay. *The Small House Book.* Boyes Hot Springs, CA: Tumbleweed Tiny House Company, 2009.

About the Author

Chris Schapdick spent decades in a lucrative career in the online media sector working in various management capacities for publicly traded corporations as well as small startups. But professional success felt hollow and failed to provide him with real purpose and deeper meaning. In 2016, Chris bid his corporate career farewell and decided to strike out on his own, launching several businesses designed around building tiny houses and coaching others to follow their dreams of a simpler lifestyle. Chris now splits his time between northern New Jersey, where he lives with his teenage daughter, and the Catskills region of New York State, where he owns and manages his businesses. It is in the solitude of the forest and rolling hills that he finds the inspiration and creative energy that fuel his designs and projects. Chris is a sought-after blogger and speaker on the tiny house circuit

Photo credit: Mia Fitzmaurice

and has garnered awards for his builds, including "Best Tiny House in New Jersey" at the United Tiny House Association's New Jersey Tiny House Festival (2017) as well as in November 2017 at the same organization's event in Florida.

Photo Credits

All photos by Chris Schapdick unless otherwise noted. All illustrations conceived by Chris Schapdick and created by David Fisk. The following images are credited to their respective creators: page 4: Eileen Fitzmaurice; page 173: Mia Fitzmaurice; pages 162 bottom, 164 top, and 167: Emily and Dan Moore. The following images are credited to Shutterstock.com and their respective creators: front cover (sky): sumroeng chinnapan; front cover (bushes): Snufkin_79; front cover (grass): Krivosheev Vitaly; back cover (sky): Ariel Celeste Photography; page 29: Ariel Celeste Photography; page 30: Claire Slingerland; page 31: Artazum; pages 56–57: Odua Images; page 159: Vyaseleva Elena; page 160 right: Filtered Photons; page 166 top: Lighttraveler; page 168: snancys; page 169: inrainbows

Index

BUILDING YOUR TINY HOUSE DREAM

Additional Praise

"If you've fantasized about what it would be like to downsize, big-time, *Building Your Tiny House Dream* lets you road test the idea…literally. You'll need some tools and carpentry skills, but author Chris Schapdick—who built his own tiny house and now an even tinier one on wheels—walks you through each and every step, with pictures all along the way. Whether you follow his design or create your own, he also shares helpful advice about incorporating key storage and squeezing in a kitchen and, amazingly, bathroom, along with fun finishing touches. Window boxes and a Dutch door on a camper? Yes, please!"

—Janet Mowat, Editorial Director, Parade Media

"Chris Schapdick's *Building Your Tiny House Dream* will at the very least inspire more people to take that often-difficult first step toward building something. And, at best, it will bring a little beauty into the world."

—Ken Clark, Editor-in-Chief,
Hardware & Building Supply Dealer

"I'm a huge fan of Chris and his builds! I've gotten lots of inspiration from both and can't wait to see how his new book equips others to build their tiny house dream."

—Chris Strathy, The Capable Carpenter

"*Building Your Tiny House Dream* is a practical manual for simpler living. And it empowers anyone with this dream—not just those with a garage full of expensive tools or a lifetime of carpentry experience. Leaning on Schapdick's rich experience in the field, his latest book serves as a source of inspiration as much as technical guidance. It's the perfect starting place for someone getting serious about a tiny house."

—Aaron Bible, Writer, *Elevation Outdoors*, *Men's Health*,
Backpacker, *Outdoor Retailer*, and more

"I am a self-identified Tiny House Lover, even though I don't live in one myself (yet!). After reading Chris Schapdick's excellent *Building Your Tiny House Dream*, I now feel that it just might be possible! Chris' combination of enthusiasm and expertise comes across in these pages. He guides the reader through the step-by-step process of planning and building your tiny house dream. The use of photographs, illustrations, tables, and how-to instructions makes this guide a must-have for the tiny house dreamer. Chris integrates his inspiring personal story with an overview of the tiny house scene and the details for your DIY project. Pick up a copy of this informative and easy-to-follow guide and start dreaming!"

—Felicia Tomasko, Editor-in-Chief *LA YOGA Magazine*;
Editorial Director Bliss Network

"After reading this fun and in-depth look at the process of building a tiny home, it actually feels doable! I love the idea of creating a space for an additional home office, pool house, or she-shed. I see a lot of bespoke design and it's exciting to imagine creating a really custom space for myself or my family. Thank you to Chris Schapdick for doing the hard work of figuring out all the details for us!"

—Lynette Hebble, Editor,
San Diego PREMIER Properties & Lifestyles

"How apt of a title by Chris. Since I first met him he has been turning dreams into reality. His livable art isn't so much about being tiny as it is about being intelligent and functional. He understands how to keep dreams from turning into nightmares and he is amazing at expressing that sentiment. I can't wait to dive into this one!"

—Andrew Odom, *Tiny House Magazine*